Keeping the PEACE

THE ALDERMASTON STORY

A brief account of the first fifty years
of the home of Britain's nuclear deterrent,
The Atomic Weapons Establishment, Aldermaston

David J. Hawkings

First published in Great Britain in 2000
in association with AWE Plc
Leo Cooper
an imprint of
Pen and Sword Books Ltd
47 Church Street
Barnsley
South Yorkshire
S70 2AS

© Crown copyright 2000

ISBN 0 85052 775 9

Designed by AWE Media and Publishing Group

Printed in England by
The Bath Press, Bath

Contents

Chapter		Page No.
	Foreword	1
1	The Dawn of an Era	3
2	Coming Home	11
3	From Airfield to 'Atom Factory'	17
4	A Diversity of Skills	23
5	Something in the Air	29
	Capturing the moment	35
	Testing Times	36
6	Going Thermonuclear	37
7	Lasting Partnerships	45
8	The Early Weapons	51
9	WE 177 and Beyond - New Generations of Weapons	57
10	Prohibited Places	63
	Campaigning Days	69
	Taking no Chances	70
11	Swords into Ploughshares	71
12	Winds of Change	79
13	A Safe and Good Neighbour	85
14	After the Cold War - the Making of a Modern Laboratory	95
15	Towards the Next Fifty Years	105
	Timeline	111

Foreword

For half a century, the Atomic Weapons Establishment at Aldermaston has been at the heart of Britain's nuclear deterrent.

During all this period, Aldermaston's scientists and engineers have worked at the leading edge of science and technology to design, build and test a range of nuclear warheads which have formed the basis of the UK's strategic deterrent and which, without doubt, in the hands of the Royal Navy and Royal Air Force have made a vital contribution to 'Keeping the Peace'.

Much has changed on the global stage since that raw April day in 1950, when the transition from wartime airfield to nuclear weapons laboratory first began. Yet, from the pioneering atmospheric tests of the 1950s, through the period of underground tests, to our current post Cold War era, AWRE Aldermaston, together with its factories and outstations, has made a unique contribution to Britain's nuclear deterrent.

For fifty years successive Governments have looked to AWE to maintain the nuclear arsenal in a safe and effective way whilst minimising the impact on the environment. In recent years the task has been to withdraw weapons from the stockpile, to develop ways of verifying performance and safety without recourse to live testing and to advise the international community on the vital issue of test ban verification.

Other recent developments have been the introduction of 'Government Owned Contractor Operated' management arrangements for AWE with external licensing by the Nuclear Installations Inspectorate and the development of a community relations programme, reflecting the greater spirit of openness which now prevails.

'Keeping the Peace' does not pretend to be the official history of Britain's nuclear deterrent. Rather, it paints a fascinating picture of a unique institution and its work during the past fifty years. I am sure there is something here for everyone interested in the UK nuclear weapons programme.

G.N.Beaven
Director General Submarines and
Chief Strategic Systems Executive

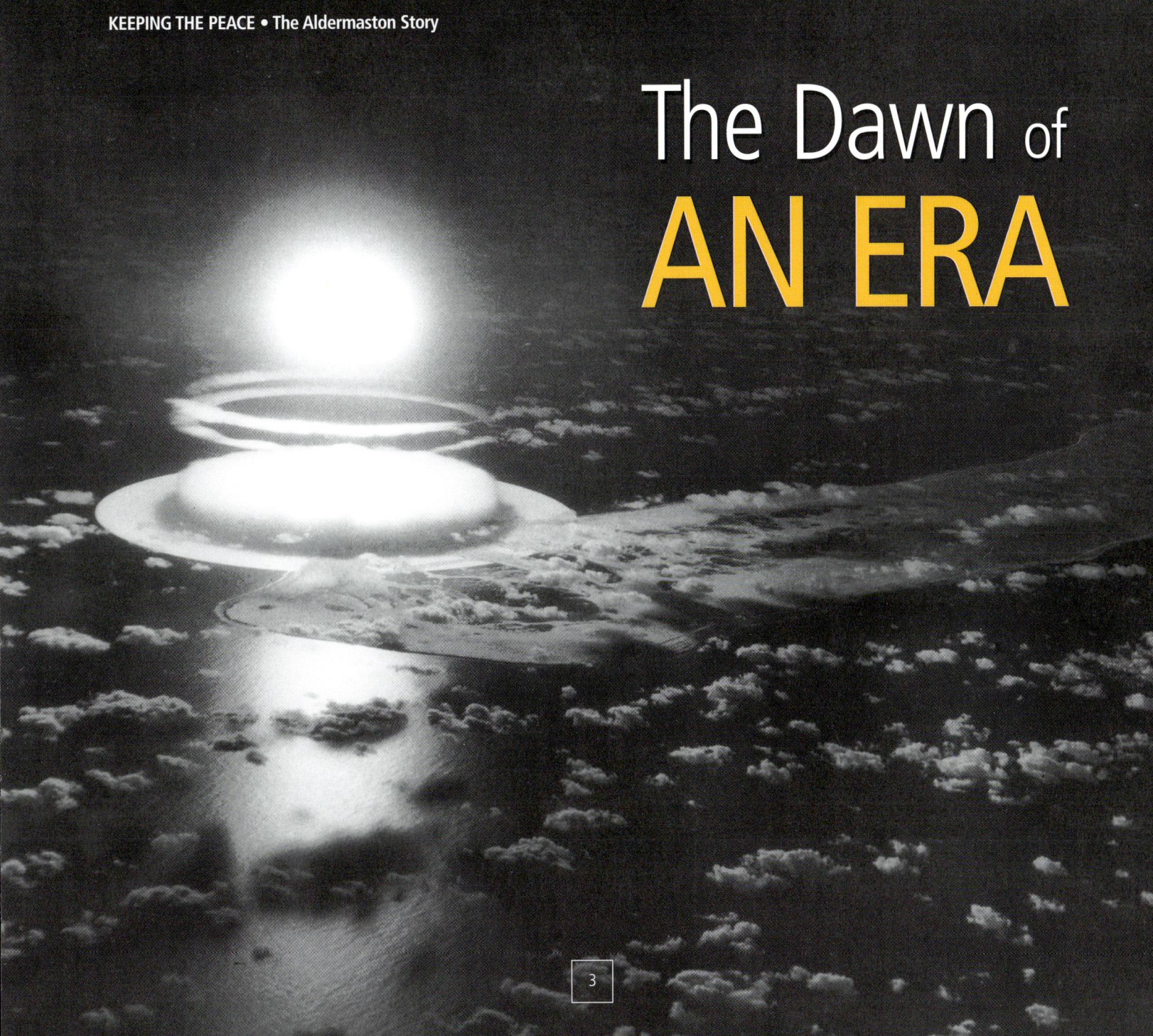

KEEPING THE PEACE • The Aldermaston Story

The Dawn of
AN ERA

Chapter 1

The Dawn of an Era

On a bleak day in the early Spring of 1950, a wartime airfield in southern England was being prepared for a new and singular role. From here, the US Army Airforce had launched their Waco and Horsa gliders to support the D-Day landings in 1944; now, with peace won, the site was poised to take on a new role of global importance - securing that peace through nuclear deterrence.

The story of Britain's rise to become a nuclear power had begun early in the twentieth century, when British scientists played a leading part in the international development of the new science of atomic physics, with Rutherford succeeding in 'splitting the atom' as early as 1919 and James Chadwick identifying the sub-atomic particle, the neutron in 1931. There was much speculation about the potential of atomic energy which, if it could be released, might be used as a power source, or for a 'superbomb'.

In 1938, German scientists Hahn and Strassman, working at the Kaiser Wilhelm Institute for Chemistry in Berlin observed strange reactions in uranium. This work was to prove to be the key to

◀ The shock wave from one of the British *Grapple-Z* nuclear tests advances across Christmas Island in September 1958. The atmospheric tests conducted in the 1950s were the culmination of research started more than ten years before.

the design of nuclear weapons, although initially, the findings were not fully understood. They were interpreted by their former colleague, the Austrian Lise Meitner and her nephew, Otto Frisch, who realized that a new process had been identified, which they called 'nuclear fission'. Their conclusions appeared in the journal *Nature* early in 1939 and naturally excited scientists across the world, who began to investigate the possibilities of a chain reaction in uranium. But there seemed to be an insuperable problem: tons of uranium would be needed to sustain a chain reaction.

Ironically, it was two refugees from Nazi Germany who provided the breakthrough. By March 1940, Otto Frisch and Rudolf Peierls, then Professor of Mathematical Physics at Birmingham University, had produced two brief papers which would rank amongst the most significant documents of the twentieth century. They argued that if the rare isotope uranium 235 could be separated, the amount needed for an atomic bomb could be measured in kilos rather than tons. If the fissile component of the weapon was made in two parts each less than the critical mass, the bomb could be set off simply by bringing the two parts rapidly together.

'...The energy liberated by a 5kg bomb would be equivalent to... several thousand tons of dynamite...' the memorandum claimed.

Greatly interested, the British Government formed the so-called 'Maud Committee' to co-ordinate further research into the authors' astounding claims. The committee members included leading British scientists and reported direct to the Air Ministry and later to the Ministry of Aircraft Production.

In July 1941, the Maud Committee issued two reports. The first, *On the Use of Uranium for a Bomb* concluded that the weapon suggested by Frisch and Peierls would definitely work and that it could be made by the end of 1943. In a prophetic final paragraph the authors said: '...*the scheme for a uranium bomb is practicable and likely to lead to decisive results in the war*'. The report made detailed recommendations on the plant needed for the large scale separation of U 235 and even gave cost estimates.

The second report *On the use of Uranium as a Source of Power* referred to the work being carried out at the Cavendish Laboratories in Cambridge: it was discovered that a by-product of the operations of nuclear reactors would be 'element 94', soon to be known as plutonium, and that one of its isotopes (239) would have similar characteristics to uranium 235. Furthermore, it could be extracted chemically from the uranium fuel more easily than the separation of U 235.

▼ The opening paragraphs of the *'Memorandum on the properties of a radioactive "super-bomb"'*. Dated March 1940, it helped convince the British Government to develop nuclear weapons.

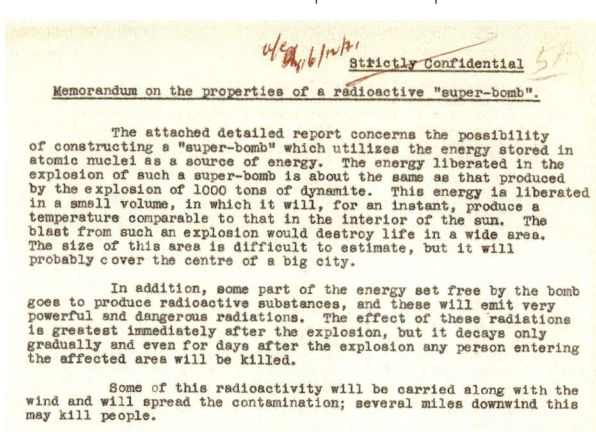

At the same time, an American dimension to the work was being developed; in the Autumn of 1940 the Air Ministry Scientific Advisor, Henry Tizard, had been sent to Washington with the atomic scientist John Cockcroft. With them went details of the latest British scientific and technical secrets including innovations such as the jet engine and the cavity magnetron, which led to vital improvements in the performance of radar.

Tizard wanted to attract American interest in the way science was being harnessed to the British war effort. If successful, Churchill hoped it would lead to American aid in the dire struggle developing against Germany. By late 1940, exchanges of nuclear information were in progress, visiting Americans being impressed by British work on the bomb. The reports of the Maud Committee were of immense influence in the USA. At a meeting in the White

Chapter 1

House in October 1941, the Presidential decision was taken which led to the establishment of the Manhattan Project.

Nevertheless, Britain had briefly held the world lead in the development of this awesome new technology and in October 1941, began the world's first atomic weapons research programme under the code name *Tube Alloys*. The team of scientists directed by Wallace (later Sir Wallace) Akers, who had been released from his job as Research Director at Imperial Chemical Industries, set to work in the requisitioned Shell Mex building in London. Their principal challenge was to design a plant to produce the enriched uranium required for the fissile core of a nuclear weapon.

The attack on Pearl Harbor in December 1941 had given American atom bomb research further momentum. But in Britain the growing demands of the *Tube Alloys* project and the wartime lack of resources were hampering progress and the government reluctantly concluded that its own work could only continue as part of the American programme. So, under the Quebec Agreement of August 1943, *Tube Alloys* was shelved and Britain became a junior partner with America; of the forty scientists and engineers assigned to the Manhattan project under mission leader Professor James Chadwick, nineteen were at the newly created Los Alamos Laboratory in New Mexico.

Amongst the British scientists assigned to the Manhattan Project were Sir Geoffrey Taylor, a world authority on fluid mechanics, who had been carrying out research for the British Government into the blast waves caused by high explosives, the Australian Mark Oliphant, renowned for his work on sub-atomic particles, James Tuck, Neils Bohr, Rudolf Peierls and Klaus Fuchs, later to be convicted of espionage. Also at Los Alamos was a young scientist called William Penney, who was destined to play a vital part in the Aldermaston story. Penney had worked with Taylor on the Government's Physics of Explosives Committee and he soon realised that Penney's expertise on the behaviour of shock waves would be of value to the Manhattan Project.

◀ William Penney headed the Pressure Group (Cans and Drums) during the American nuclear tests at Bikini Atoll in 1946 - Operation *Crossroads*. Here, five gallon cans placed on a ship have been crushed by the pressure from the Bikini Able shot on 1 July 1946. The degree of crushing enabled the approximate yield of the device to be calculated.

Graduating from Imperial College in 1929 with a first class degree achieved in just two years, Penney went on to gain an MA at the University of Wisconsin in America and by 1933 had won a scholarship to Pembroke College Cambridge. His first academic appointment was as assistant professor of mathematics at Imperial College. As part of his war work, Penney had studied the effects of waves on the Mulberry Harbours being planned for the Allied invasion of Europe. The result was the Bombardon, a floating steel breakwater which sheltered the massive invasion forces off the Normandy coast.

The challenge facing the Manhattan Project was to produce weapons using the man-made element plutonium. The simple uranium 235 device outlined in the Frisch-Peierls Memorandum led initially to the adoption of a 'gun-assembly' design. The principle of the design was simple: two pieces of fissile material, each of a sub-critical size were brought together using conventional explosives, their combined mass being sufficient to start a chain reaction.

However, by 1944 it had been predicted that this technique would be unsuitable for a plutonium bomb as there was a risk of premature detonation. The value of the British contribution to the development of an alternative design - the 'implosion method' - is clear from a Los Alamos document of the time which specifically named Fuchs, Peierls and Tuck as joint inventors or significant contributors to the new technique. In the implosion method, a fissile core is surrounded by specially shaped 'lenses' of high explosive which, when detonated in a specific way, compress the core to a point where it achieves a critical mass, so starting a chain reaction. Vital to the success of the implosion method was the design of the explosives and detonators.

The Manhattan Project culminated in the dropping of atomic bombs on Japan in August 1945, bringing the Second World War to an abrupt end. *Little Boy*, detonated over Hiroshima on 6 August 1945 was a gun device; *Fat Man*, detonated over Nagasaki three days later was an implosion weapon. The results were decisive: as the British Official History says, *'...the atomic bomb had shown itself to be the supreme weapon which could terrify into instant submission a country which did not possess it...'* Observing the Nagasaki event from the photographic aircraft *Full House* were Britain's William Penney and Group Captain Leonard Cheshire, the legendary RAF bomber pilot.

Back in Britain, the foundations of a nuclear weapons industry were being laid. In December 1945 a Committee under Prime Minister Clement Attlee ordered the construction of an atomic pile to produce plutonium and a report on Britain's requirement for atomic bombs.

Penney had returned to Britain by the end of 1945; shortly after, he was approached by the novelist C.P. Snow, then working as a Civil Service Commissioner, to take up the post of Chief Superintendent Armament Research, based at Fort Halstead in Kent. Reluctantly Penney turned away from the promising academic career which beckoned and his appointment as CSAR was

Chapter 1

The US Bikini Baker shot rises above the atoll on 25 July 1946. An armada of more than sixty surplus warships was moored in the area as part of a target response study. Following his role in Operation *Crossroads*, Penney was appointed Scientific Advisor to the British representative at the US Atomic Energy Commission.

announced on 1 January 1946. As CSAR, Penney was responsible for all types of armaments research and it was to be some time before he began work on the British nuclear weapon. However, his work took him back to the USA, where he formed part of the team preparing for the American nuclear tests at Bikini Atoll. Later that year, Penney was appointed Scientific Advisor to the British Representative at the United Nations Atomic Energy Commission. The scene had been set; now, the question was: should Britain take the ultimate decision to proceed with its own nuclear deterrent?

The passing of the Atomic Energy Act (known as the McMahon Act) by the United States in 1946 had (among other things) placed severe restrictions on information about nuclear weapons. Apart from Penney's involvement with the trials at Bikini, it stopped co-operation between Britain and America on nuclear weapon design at a stroke. But if anything, the decision had strengthened Britain's determination to build her own atomic bomb. For some months the international situation was fluid, but by the end of 1946 it was clear that the United Nations' efforts to introduce a system of international control of nuclear weapons had failed and the Americans had ruled out a joint US/UK nuclear programme.

British frustration at being excluded from collaboration with the United States came to a head at a Cabinet Committee meeting in October 1946; the Chancellor of the Exchequer and the President of the Board of Trade objected to spending the £30 million or so needed to build the gaseous diffusion plant Britain would need to produce the U 235 for her own bomb. Ernest Bevin, the Foreign Secretary, rounded on them and snorted: *'We have got to have this thing over here whatever it costs...[and] we've got to have the bloody Union Jack on it'*.

The die was cast and in January 1947 the British Government under Prime Minister Clement Attlee authorized the development of nuclear weapons.

By this time, the Government had already set up, in late 1945, a general purpose Atomic Energy Research Establishment at Harwell under Dr. John Cockcroft and - early in 1946 - a production organization based at Risley under Christopher Hinton. In July 1947 the Government announced that it had chosen a site for plutonium production: Windscale on the coast of Cumberland. Work began almost at once and by June 1951 both piles had gone critical. Design of the first weapon (a plutonium bomb) began in June 1947 at Fort Halstead in Kent under William Penney. His group, located in a secret enclave within the Armaments Research Establishment, was known simply as 'High Explosive Research' - HER.

Of the British scientists who had worked at Los Alamos, only Penney went on to HER. However several of his former at Los Alamos colleagues made significant contributions to the project. This was hardly surprising - as the head of the British Mission, Sir James Chadwick, pointed out, ' ... *British scientists ... could not be expected to take amnesia tablets before returning home'*.

Chapter 1

▲ The cavity magnetron, which heralded improvements in radar, was one of the British inventions which led to exchanges of nuclear weapons information between Britain and the US during the Second World War.
Picture: Science Museum/Science and Society Picture library

◀ Otto Frisch (L) and Rudolf Peierls (R), authors of the 1940 memorandum on the military use of nuclear energy - one of the most significant documents of the twentieth century.
Picture: Science Museum/Science and Society Picture library

▲ Sir John Cockcroft, pictured in 1932 with atom smashing apparatus he designed with Ernest Walton. A later version of the device played an important part in the research carried out at Aldermaston in the 1950s.
Picture: Science Museum/Science and Society Picture library

▲ *Fat Man*, the weapon detonated over Nagasaki on 9 August 1945. Its 'implosion' design formed the basis for all the weapons in the UK's nuclear stockpile.

◀ This monument marks the 'Trinity Site' where the world's first atom bomb was tested on 16 July 1945 at Alamagordo, New Mexico. British scientists played an important role in the Manhattan Project which culminated in the explosion of the "Trinity" device.

KEEPING THE PEACE • The Aldermaston Story

Coming
HOME

Chapter 2

Coming Home

As HER's work on the nuclear bomb began to gather momentum, it was realized that such a major project would need a home of its own away from the Armaments Research Establishment at Fort Halstead.

And so began the search for a permanent home for Britain's nuclear weapons programme. Several former airfields in Wiltshire and Gloucestershire were considered, with a site at South Cerney being selected by Penney. In the event, the Air Ministry did not wish to part with it, so the hunt was on again, with sites in South Wales and Shropshire being investigated. None was suitable; eventually, on the recommendation of the Ministry of Civil Aviation, a wartime airfield site in Berkshire, some sixty miles from London, was selected.

The quiet village nearby was soon to become a household word: 'Aldermaston' - the home of Britain's nuclear deterrent. Aldermaston village has a long history: recorded in Domesday Book as 'Aeldremanestone', the village clustered around a crossing point on the River Kennet, surrounded by wooded slopes and fertile meadows. Not far away was the Roman provincial capital of Silchester, whose outer defences - the fifth century 'Grim's Bank' - extended to within the airfield site itself.

◀ The old airfield layout is still visible as construction of AWRE gets underway in 1951.

The cluster of redbrick cottages and modestly elegant houses, overlooked by a twelfth century church and an imposing manor house seemed an unlikely location for a major new industry.

After the Second World War, Aldermaston had been chosen as the site for a central flying school, where more than 1000 former RAF pilots were trained to fly civil aircraft. Many of the wartime buildings were refurbished and improved runway lighting was installed. In 1947, Aldermaston was designated a temporary civil airport by the Ministry of Civil Aviation and was for a while considered as a possible site for London's third airport. In April 1947, the training school was incorporated into the British national airlines, BOAC and BEA. Navigation and communications systems were installed and a Link Trainer was in use. But the School was losing money and its operations were scaled down. On 30 September 1948, all training had ceased and Aldermaston prepared to play its next role.

In 1950 the area, although no more than a dozen miles from the surrounding towns of Basingstoke, Newbury and Reading, was remote and thinly populated. Yet local people seemed prepared to accept the radical development on their doorstep: Aldermaston's vicar, the Reverend Frederick Newham simply commented: *'If atomic research has to be done, it may as well be done here'*. A note of caution was sounded by Bradfield parish council, which recorded its opinion that *'we don't want a potential danger spot bang in the middle of our district.... but we must accept it with as a good a grace as we can'*.

The building firm W.E. Chivers and Sons, which had constructed the Atomic Energy Authority's site at Harwell, won the contract for converting the windswept airfield into the Atomic Weapons Research Establishment. Under the Direction of the Ministry of Works, which had formally taken possession of the site on 1 April 1950, they embarked on an intensive building programme. By 1952, some 3,600 labourers, many of them Irish, Polish and Scots, were living in temporary camps in nearby Tadley. Work continued day and night to complete buildings A1.1, A3 and A6, which were essential to the construction of the first nuclear test device.

By the spring of 1952, the most important of these, building A 1.1, was handed over; Aldermaston stood ready to cast the plutonium which would form the fissile assembly of Britain's first nuclear device. This was the culmination of a remarkable effort; building work had continued day and night; not only were production facilities and laboratories needed, a major project was the construction of a twelve mile pipeline to the River Thames near Pangbourne, to discharge treated liquid effluent.

▼ The RAF formally hand over Aldermaston Airfield to the US Army Air Force in August 1942. AWE's Falcon Gate now occupies this site.

From 1950 to the end of 1952, some work continued at Fort Halstead; indeed, Penney was not formally appointed as AWRE's first Director until December 1953. However, there were practical problems in controlling activities on two sites separated by more than sixty miles, which were made worse by the intensive building programme at Aldermaston; this had transformed the former airfield into a vast construction site. The seas of mud, the contractors' huts and the scurrying labour force gave at least one employee the impression of a 'Romany Camp'.

But by the time of the election of a Conservative government under Prime Minister Winston Churchill in October 1951, at political level the heady

Chapter 2

Hundreds of gliders were launched from Aldermaston in support of the Normandy Landings in 1944; here, Wacos (foreground) and Horsas (rear) are marshalled ready for flight.

pioneering days were almost over. Even whilst work on the first test device was underway at Aldermaston, Churchill wrote cautiously to the Paymaster General, Lord Cherwell: *'I have never wished since our decision during the war that England should start the manufacture of atomic bombs. Research however must be energetically pursued. We should have the art rather than the article'*.

In the event, Aldermaston was to deliver both.

For the staff at Aldermaston it was a time of unprecedented energy and enthusiasm. Whilst laboratories and offices were being constructed on site, many scientific staff and construction workers lived in hostels - grandly named 'Residential Clubs' - at Grazeley Green and Clay Hill near the Royal Ordnance Factory at Burghfield. And the village of Tadley, just across the county boundary in Hampshire, was transformed as a four-hundred bedroom hostel (replacing earlier Service accommodation) and hundreds of houses rose on the pine clad heathland around the site.

One of the first to be built was Heather House, intended as the home for William Penney, AWRE's first Director. Set in three acres of wooded grounds, it soon became the focal point for the families moving into the new estates in Tadley and Baughurst. The Director's wife, an experienced nurse, helped build a community spirit with her support for the many young mothers, weighing babies and handing out orange juice. Day and evening classes were held at Heather House too, as well as sewing sessions for the wives of the ever growing number of employees 'inside the wire'.

Even today it is possible to sense something of the community spirit which grew up around AWRE - some fifty per cent of Aldermaston's employees still live within five miles of the site. With its own shops, clubs and cinema, it was not long before the media dubbed Tadley 'Atom Town'. Yet much has changed; Heather House passed into private ownership in 1965 and slowly declined until destroyed by fire in 1995. Boundary Hall Hostel and the Cinema Royal are no more and most of the 'Authority Houses' are now owner occupied. But the neat avenues and generous open spaces laid out with such hope in the 1950s remain as a testament to the huge change which AWRE brought to this quiet corner of north Hampshire.

Heather House, Heath End, Tadley, ▶ pictured here in 1965, was built for AWRE's first Director, William Penney, in 1951.

Chapter 2

▲ Civilian radio engineers under training at the Airways Training School, set up at Aldermaston Airfield in 1947 by the national airlines BOAC and BEA. This short lived venture ceased operations in September 1948.

▲ Members of the West Berks Parachute Regiment Association proudly parade by the D-Day Memorial erected outside AWE's main administration building F6.1, on 6 June 1994.

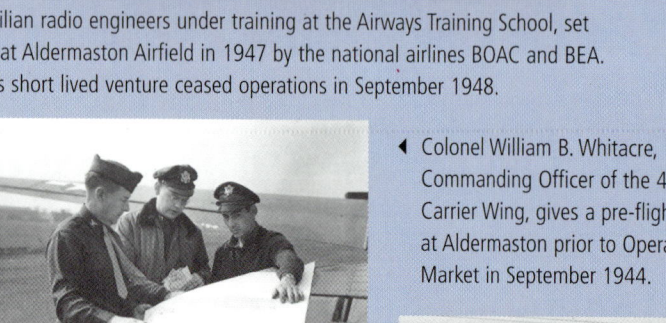

◀ Colonel William B. Whitacre, Commanding Officer of the 434 Troop Carrier Wing, gives a pre-flight briefing at Aldermaston prior to Operation Market in September 1944.

▼ The UK Atomic Energy Authority built nearly two thousand houses for AWRE staff. Here "Type D" three bedroomed houses are seen under construction in Whitedown Road, Tadley, on a wintry day in 1955.

▲ Accommodation for AWRE's growing workforce was
◀ supplemented by Boundary Hall Hostel, seen here nearing completion in 1960. A focal point of the Hostel was the New Boundary Hall Club; in the above 1961 picture, AWRE staff relax after a day's work.

16

KEEPING THE PEACE • The Aldermaston Story

From Airfield to 'ATOM FACTORY'

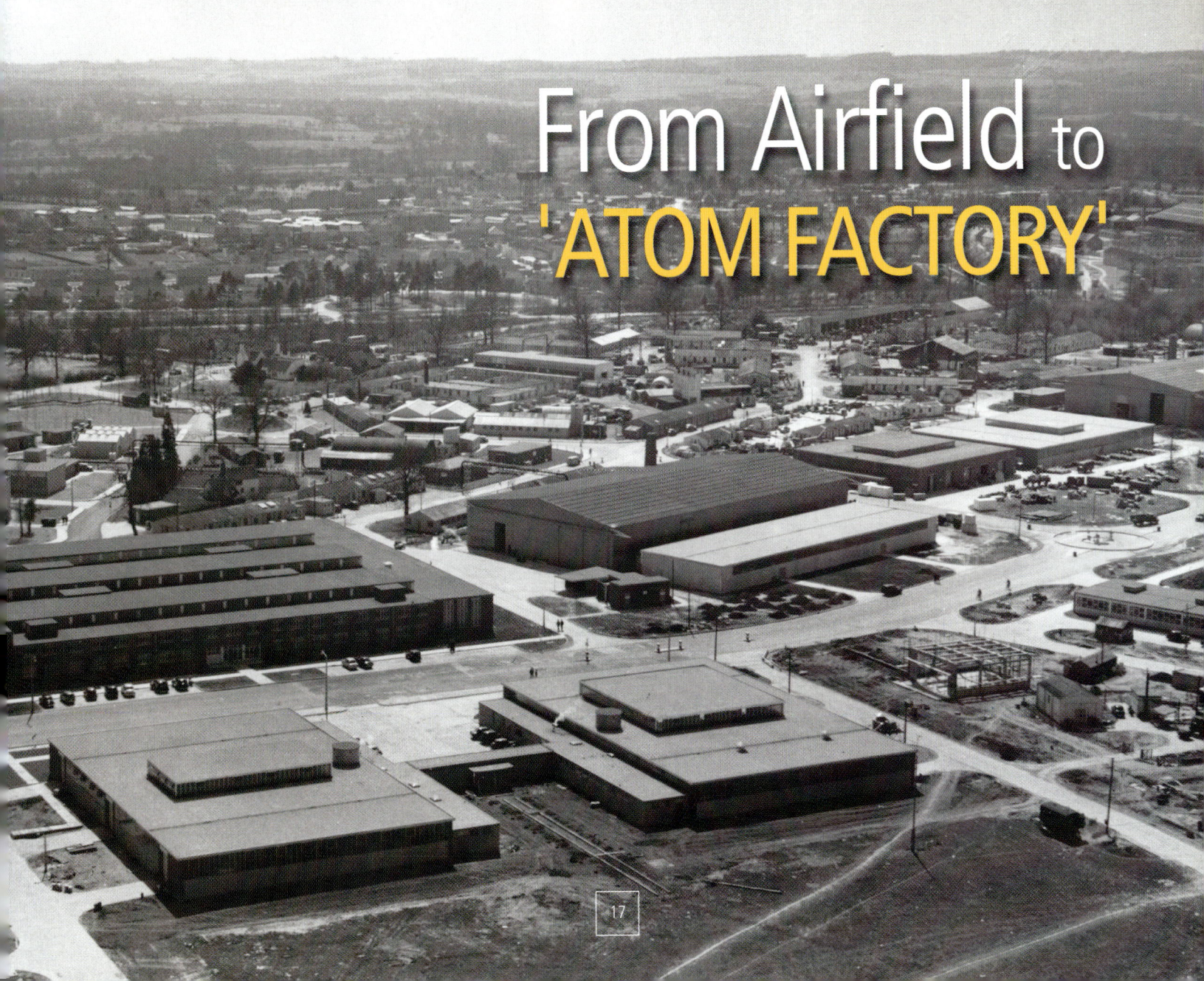

Chapter 3

From airfield to 'Atom Factory'

A glance at a recent aerial photograph of Aldermaston will reveal the tell-tale skeleton of an airfield, with straight roads - the former runways and taxiways - at opposing angles and the metal roofs of vast hangars. During the 1950s and 1960s much of that existing infrastructure was used in support of the nuclear programme. The hangars and airfield buildings were quickly taken over as stores, offices and workshops. There were many new buildings, too, designed and constructed to serve their unique purpose.

To cope with the demands of the design, trials and manufacturing programmes for an expanding arsenal of weapons, AWRE's workforce grew rapidly, peaking at nearly 9,000 employees in 1962.

The manufacture of the fissile components from plutonium and highly enriched uranium took place in purpose built facilities and in addition to production a wide range of research projects were developed. As part of Britain's growing nuclear programme, both civil and military, Aldermaston had the opportunity to undertake research outside the closely protected confines of its nuclear weapons work. In what was then the new field of atomic energy, each of the three technical groups of the United Kingdom Atomic Energy Authority (UKAEA) was involved in basic research to extend understanding of nuclear structure and solve the vast range of problems faced by their scientists and engineers.

In his foreword to a 1955 booklet about Aldermaston aimed at science students, Aldermaston's Director, William Penney, wrote of the Atomic Energy Authority: *'All three groups have magnificent laboratories......There is a rapid and continuous flow of ideas, techniques and interests between the Groups...'* He added *'In short, the necessity for secrecy in atomic energy is proving less restrictive to the scientist than might be expected. ...AWRE will not only handle fissile metals and other "atomic" materials but will also have opportunities and facilities for basic research'*. Penney's personal view of the nuclear weapons programme was clear; he looked forward to the day when *'...the Government will be able to instruct AWRE to beat the atomic bombs into nuclear power stations'*.

◀ By 1953, the wartime hangars had been joined by new laboratories and workshops. The growing town of Tadley can be seen in the distance.

Meanwhile, Aldermaston's principal function - the design and production of nuclear weapons - called for a mix of scientific disciplines and associated facilities. They included mathematical and experimental physics to determine, for example, the behaviour of neutrons in the unique environment of a nuclear explosion, and astrophysics to understand the behaviour of matter at the huge temperatures generated in such a blast - hotter than the centre of the sun.

In order to provide the military with the weapons it required, Aldermaston's scientists had to be able to predict with great accuracy the complex processes within an atomic explosion. Supplementing the theory was a wide range of experimental physics. This included techniques for producing and counting high intensity short duration neutron pulses, mass spectrometers for metallurgical and environmental studies, scintillators for measuring nuclear radiations and shock tubes for analysing the propagation of shock waves.

The development of suitable high explosives to compress the fissile core required the attention not only of Aldermaston's physicists to study the development of shock waves but of its chemists, to develop explosives of the highest possible power

▼ A traditional method in use to fabricate the decorative panels for the N62 tower (see picture on p.22). The motorcycle so carefully posed in the background on this April day in 1958 is a 500cc Sunbeam.

compatible with safety. Radiochemical analysis of nuclear test samples was used to determine the yield of the test device and the technique was also developed to support the new discipline of radiation measurement and health physics; much work was done at Aldermaston to improve the accuracy of routine monitoring.

And to record and measure the results not only from experiments conducted on site, but also the effects of actual nuclear tests, old techniques were improved and new ones developed; amongst these were ultra high speed oscillography, very high

Chapter 3

speed gamma flux measurements and ultra high speed photography. They were all essential tools in Aldermaston's quest to understand better the atomic forces it was studying.

The inclusion of a wide range of unusual materials in a nuclear warhead requires a deep understanding of the properties of metals; metallurgy has therefore always been of great significance at Aldermaston. By the mid 1950s, techniques for working uranium and beryllium were being developed, including powder production and sintering. Much fundamental work on plutonium was carried out which called for the development of techniques not required in more conventional metallurgy. By 1960, Aldermaston's metallurgists were making important contributions to an international conference on plutonium held in Grenoble.

Supporting the research were the weapons planners and designers, engineering services and trials division who were responsible for making the scientists' needs a reality.

As new buildings were constructed to meet those needs, Aldermaston's distinctive skyline emerged: two and three storey office and laboratory blocks, the saw-toothed roofs of the production and assembly buildings, the brutalist bulk of the bomb chambers and the towers needed to house the accelerators needed for nuclear research. Tall ventilation stacks pierced the sky whilst the gantries needed to carry services and waste products threaded their way between an ever growing complex of buildings.

◀ The fissile material processing building A45, pictured shortly after completion in May 1956.

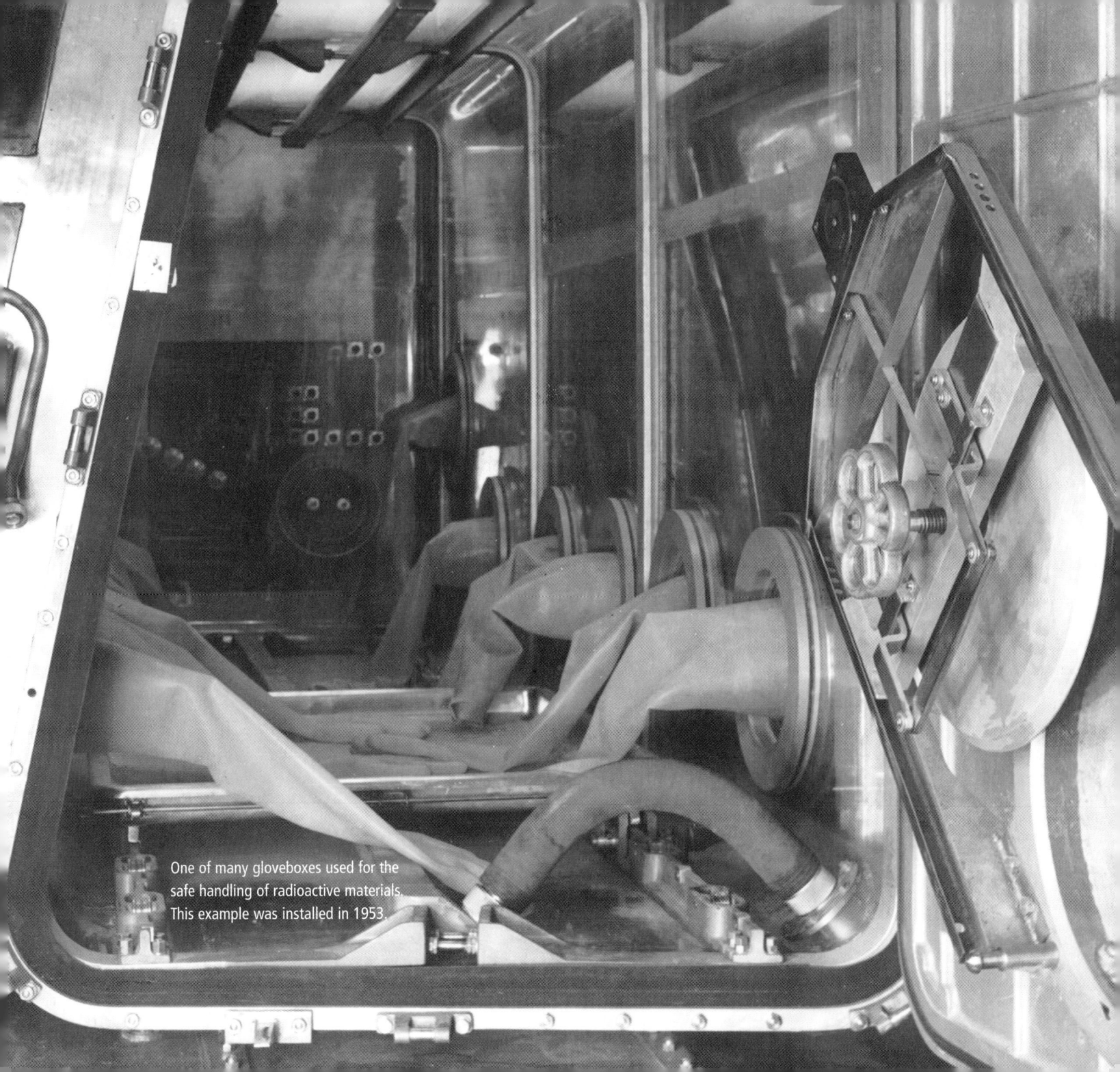

One of many gloveboxes used for the safe handling of radioactive materials. This example was installed in 1953.

Chapter 3

Echoes of the 'Festival of Britain' style in the canopy outside building A45, pictured in 1956.

The 'bomb chamber', H1, under construction in July 1954. Note the circular ports, through which high speed cameras would observe the experiments conducted inside.

A newly completed radiochemistry laboratory in A37, in 1957.

By 1958, this massive pressure vessel containing a 12 MeV tandem accelerator, was installed in building N62.

An explosives laboratory under construction in 'B Area' in March 1955.

The N62 tower dominates the west end of the site in this 1959 picture.

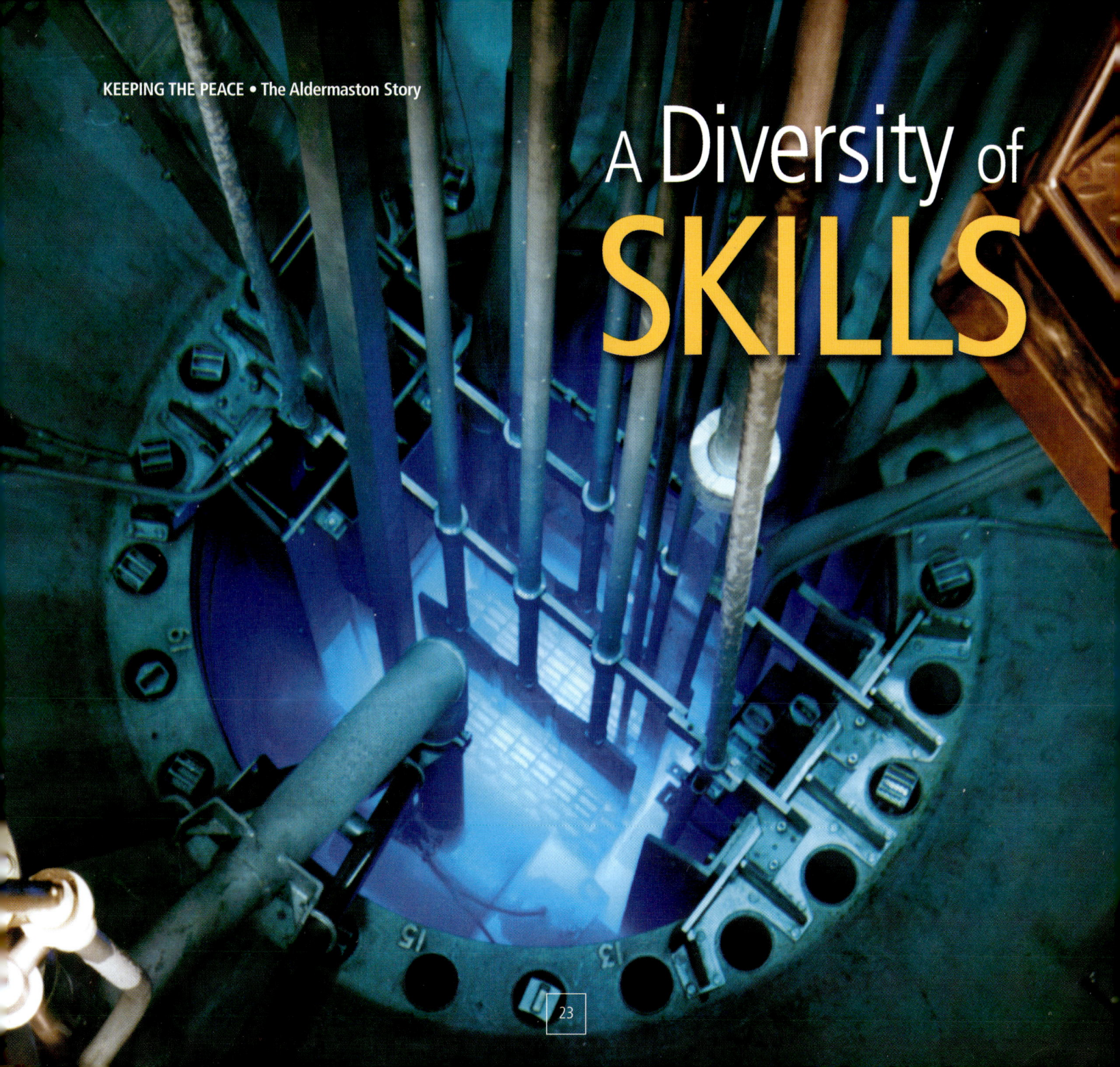

KEEPING THE PEACE • The Aldermaston Story

A Diversity of SKILLS

Chapter 4

'A Diversity of Skills'

Such was the claim made for Aldermaston in a booklet issued at the end of the 1950s. A Nuclear Research Division had been conceived at Aldermaston in early 1955 and its work was by no means limited to nuclear weapons. Particular areas of research included experimental nuclear physics, mass spectrometry, reactor physics and thermonuclear research.

Work on the controlled fusion of atoms started in 1957 using a piece of apparatus which Aldermaston's scientists christened *Oswald*. Located in building N60, it comprised a short discharge tube and a bank of 144 condensers, which were fired simultaneously to produce a current of 270,000 amps in a flash lasting just two millionths of a second. This device produced fusion neutrons six months before the ZETA reactor at Harwell was claimed to have done.

Also in N60, further controlled fusion research was being carried out. Here, the goal was to raise the temperature of deuterium (an isotope of hydrogen) to its burning point - about 100 million degrees Celsius. If deuterium could be burnt in a controlled way, a cheap and virtually inexhaustible source of power would be available. The ultimate goal of the research was to produce designs for a reactor which would eventually deliver the holy grail of limitless energy. In 1960, however, this work was transferred to the UKAEA's new site at Culham.

◀ A view into the *Herald* reactor vessel, showing the distinctive blue 'Cerenkov glow'.

▲ The *Herald* reactor under construction in 1958.

A massive 12 million volt Van de Graaff accelerator was installed in the N62 tower in support of the fusion research programme. The machine generated charged nuclear particles - ions - which could be aimed at a number of targets housed on the lower floors of the tower. The equipment allowed the study of nuclear reactions in a wide energy range. This 'hands on' approach was essential at a time when computer simulation of such events was not possible. Later, the accelerator was removed and the building was fitted with low pressure test chambers, where flight trials of components for a later generation of weapon - *Chevaline* - were carried out.

Further ion research was carried out in other buildings, including N54, where a Cockcroft-Walton accelerator was installed. This device was named after its inventors who in 1932 at the Cavendish Laboratories, first artificially split atomic nuclei by bombarding them with streams of high energy charged particles. At Aldermaston, high energy neutrons were produced by bombarding a target containing tritium atoms with a beam of deuterium ions. The operators were protected from the charged particles by concrete walls five feet thick, but could observe the experiments through a water filled window.

▼ The Cockcroft-Walton accelerator tube, pictured in 1957.

Over the years, a number of research reactors have been operated at Aldermaston. In the very early days of the nuclear programme, use was made of the reactors at Harwell and borrowed equipment, but by the mid 1950s this had become inconvenient and Aldermaston embarked on a research reactor programme of its own. The first to be built was called *Horace*; located in building R61.5 and commissioned in May 1958, it was designed as a low power facility in which various arrangements of fuel and reflector elements could be built up. Operating at just 10 watts, it was used to gain information about core behaviour and safety which could be applied to the much larger reactor *Herald*, then under construction in building R61.

Chapter 4

Neutron radiography was developed at Aldermaston as an inspection tool, for example to detect explosives in ordnance. Here, an image of a geranium shielded by two inches of lead, was produced using this technique.

KEEPING THE PEACE • The Aldermaston story

Herald was a light-water moderated and cooled pool reactor using highly enriched uranium fuel, designed to operate at a power of 5 MW. It was designed and constructed by AEI - John Thompson Nuclear Energy Ltd, who had recently completed a very similar reactor - *Merlin* , which first operated in 1959. *Merlin* and *Herald* were literally next door neighbours; AEI had built their own reactor on their site at Aldermaston Court on land which had originally been part of the Aldermaston Manor Estate, prior to its sale in 1939.

Herald - commissioned in September 1959 - gave Aldermaston a versatile research reactor; its light water moderation allowed a high neutron flux for radiation damage studies; it was also used for activation analysis, which allowed the detection of minute traces of elements, the production of isotopes for the radiochemical study of fission processes and shielding studies for health physics.

By the end of the 1960s, *Herald* was also being used extensively by universities and the Central Electricity Generating Board, whilst *Horace* was using a cold neutron source of liquid hydrogen to provide enhanced currents of cold neutrons for university research work.

The 100 watt experimental reactor *Vera* was designed for research into fast reactor physics, in particular the study of assemblies containing uranium 235 and 238. Associated with *Vera* was a high intensity pulsed neutron source and a fifty metre flight tube for measuring neutron energy spectra.

Aldermaston's fourth reactor - *Viper* - was commissioned in 1967. It is a short pulse reactor which provides neutrons for testing the vulnerability and nuclear 'hardness' of a wide variety of systems, assemblies and components. Unlike the other reactors which have been decommissioned, *Viper* is still in use, its role having extended into health physics and radiation ageing studies.

Such was the atmosphere of 'big science' in which Britain's nuclear weapons programme flourished.

Making adjustments to the core of the *Viper* ▸ reactor. Commissioned in 1967, it is the only one of Aldermaston's reactors to remain in use.

Chapter 4

With its containment vessel removed, the 6 million volt Van De Graaff accelerator is pictured in building N51. It was used to study the interaction of fast neutrons with atomic nuclei.

▲ The *Herald* reactor vessel arrives at Aldermaston on a dull day in 1958.

▼ The *Herald* reactor hall in the 1970s.

▼ A cross-section of the *Horace* reactor, commissioned in 1958.

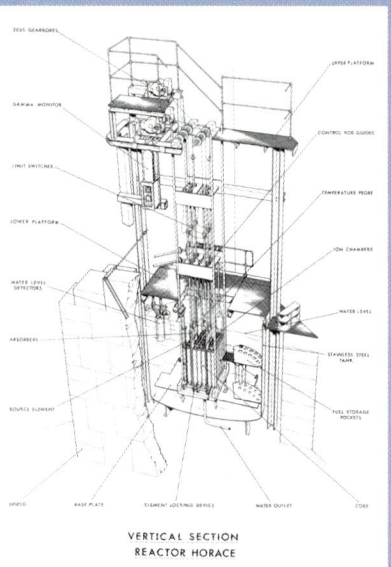

▲ The *Asp* accelerator was commissioned in 1964. It provided a source of neutrons for neutron radiography and later was used to test the vulnerability of electronic components to intense neutron fields.

KEEPING THE PEACE • The Aldermaston Story

Something in the
AIR

Chapter 5

Something in the Air

Amongst Aldermaston's chaos of construction, scientists and engineers wrestled with the many problems associated with designing and producing a test device. Codenamed *Hurricane*, Britain's first nuclear test was scheduled to take place in the Monte Bello Islands off the north west coast of Australia in October 1952.

At Woolwich, the high explosives were prepared, whilst at Windscale work was underway to produce the plutonium Aldermaston needed to cast the fissile core. In fact, the first sample of the metal to reach Aldermaston - at the end of 1951 - came from the Chalk River plant in Canada, but despite massive technical problems Windscale kept its promise to deliver sufficient metal for the test device by August 1952.

Just a few short weeks remained to prepare the fissile core. The device was to be detonated on a ship moored offshore, to simulate the effects of a nuclear weapon which had been smuggled into a British harbour; although scientific measurements would have been more easily made with the device above ground on a tower, the more 'realistic' option was chosen to ensure that as much new information as possible about nuclear blast effects would be available for civil defence purposes.

▲ This rare photograph is the only picture of the first plutonium casting to be completed in building A1.1. It was produced on 23 July 1952, only four months after the completion of the building. The hemisphere was one of two which would form the core of the *Hurricane* trial device. As the metal lay cooling, the *Hurricane* task force was steaming towards the trial site at the Monte Bello Islands, off the north west coast of Australia. The completed core was flown out to the trial site in a RAF Sunderland flying boat.

◀ The cloud from Britain's first nuclear explosion rises above the Monte Bello Islands in October 1952. Turbulent winds in the upper atmosphere twisted the cloud out of the familiar mushroom shape.

KEEPING THE PEACE • The Aldermaston story

Early in June 1952 the device, minus its plutonium core, had been loaded onto HMS *Plym*, a war surplus frigate, at Sheerness dockyard, having been transported from Foulness where it was assembled. *Plym* joined the command vessel HMS *Campania* for the ten thousand mile voyage to the test site. The fissile core was transported to the test site by air in mid September. Safely arrived and with the final preparations of the nuclear device complete, *Plym* awaited her fate. On 3 October 1952, six seconds before 9.30 am local time, the device was detonated, causing intense heat and light. The little ship had disappeared - vaporized. Britain had become a nuclear power.

▲ HMS *Plym* steams towards the Monte Bello Islands in August 1952, on the final leg of her momentous voyage.

▼ Assembling a *Blue Danube* warhead, in a still from a 1952 film made at RAE Farnborough. The device exploded in Operation *Hurricane* was very similar.

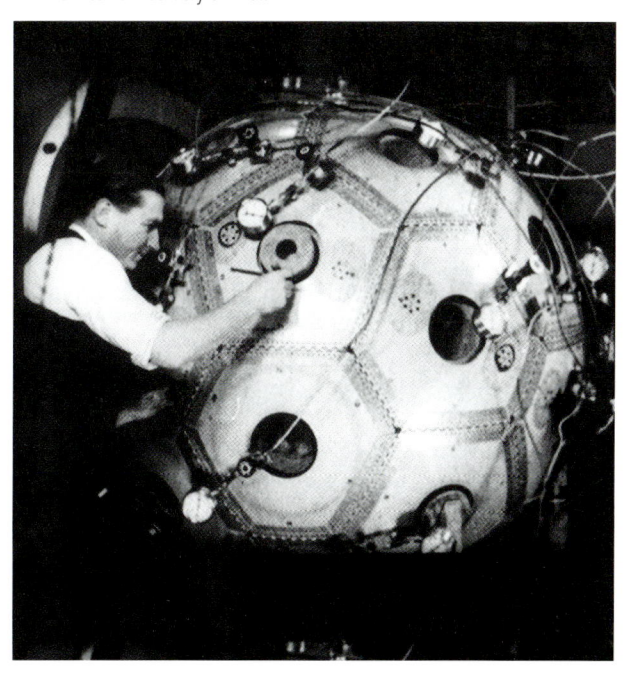

The *Hurricane* test had successfully demonstrated that Britain had mastered the design of the atom bomb; the test design was adopted as the warhead for the first nuclear weapon *Blue Danube*, of which a small stockpile was produced. Subsequent tests refined the atom bomb design: the 1953 *Totem* series at Emu Field, Woomera was designed to evaluate technical questions about the performance of plutonium 239 and to test the effects of a nuclear blast on military equipment and structures.

Chapter 5

AWRE scientists on one of the landing craft (LCMs) used to transport personnel and equipment between the islands and the support vessels. Ieuan Maddock (centre, with sunglasses) is in animated conversation with John Challens, who was in charge of preparations on HMS *Plym*. Maddock, who sent the firing signal to detonate the device, became known locally as 'The Count of Monte Bello'.

Later that year, the *Buffalo* series of tests took place at Maralinga. Four shots yielding between three and seventeen kilotons were fired over a period of twenty-six days, during which Aldermaston's scientists were plagued with bad weather. Despite the unseasonal rain the series was successful, with the first round testing the new plutonium warhead *Red Beard*, whilst round three, dropped from a Valiant bomber, was the first live ballistic test of the *Blue Danube* design.

The *Antler* series of three tests held at Maralinga in 1957 was designed to enable the production of a cheaper and operationally safer tactical nuclear weapon.

Antler was also the means of acquiring the scientific knowledge needed to produce smaller fission bombs as 'triggers' for thermonuclear megaton weapons.

This was a time of intense activity at Aldermaston; not only were innovative devices being designed, tested and evaluated, a stockpile of service warheads was being produced for the Royal Air Force. And in parallel, work was commencing on the far more powerful thermonuclear device - the hydrogen bomb, a weapon which would not have been possible without the fundamental knowledge derived from the atom bomb programme.

Sporting an Australian Army hat, William Penney arrives for Operation *Totem* in 1956. He is being greeted by his deputy, Charles Adams.

Chapter 5

Totem-like, a dummy head waits to take part in the weapon effects trials at Emu Field in 1953.

▼ A Supermarine Swift, badly damaged by the blast from one of the Operation *Buffalo* shots at Maralinga. Target response experiments were a key element of this series of trials.

▲ One of the more unusual blast effects trials on Operation *Buffalo* was to evaluate the use of telephone directories as building protection

▲ A gas mask being prepared for a weapon effects trial at Operation *Totem* in 1953.

▲ Balloons being prepared for the airburst shot at the Taranaki site at Maralinga in October 1957, during Operation *Antler*.

Charles Adams, the Trial Director, presents the commemorative plaque at the successful conclusion of Operation *Antler*. Scientific, military and administrative staff from Australia and Britain attended the event.

34

Capturing the MOMENT

The short-lived nature of nuclear phenomena has resulted in the development of many specialised techniques to record these fleeting events. High speed photography was particularly important for recording the bursts of the early atmospheric test devices. AWRE's ultra high speed Kerr-Cell cine camera exploited the properties of nitrobenzene to create an electronically activated 'shutter'; in these massive cameras, over six feet high, images were transferred to film by a mirror driven by compressed air at up to 250,000 revolutions per minute, with exposure times as short as a tenth of a microsecond.

But there were limitations - the cameras depended on high light source levels. To overcome this, AWRE started the development of photo-electrical systems; these 'image converters' rely on the property of certain metals to emit electrons in response to light or radiation.

Aldermaston has consistently been at the forefront of developments in high speed imaging. Techniques developed have included: charge coupled device (CCD)-imaging technology which enables the capture of finely detailed images of extremely transient events of nanosecond to millisecond durations; streak cameras capable of recording the shock waves in a target heated to three million degrees by Aldermaston's HELEN laser; and dual axis x-radiography of hydrodynamics experiments which can capture the key internal features of a simulated nuclear implosion.

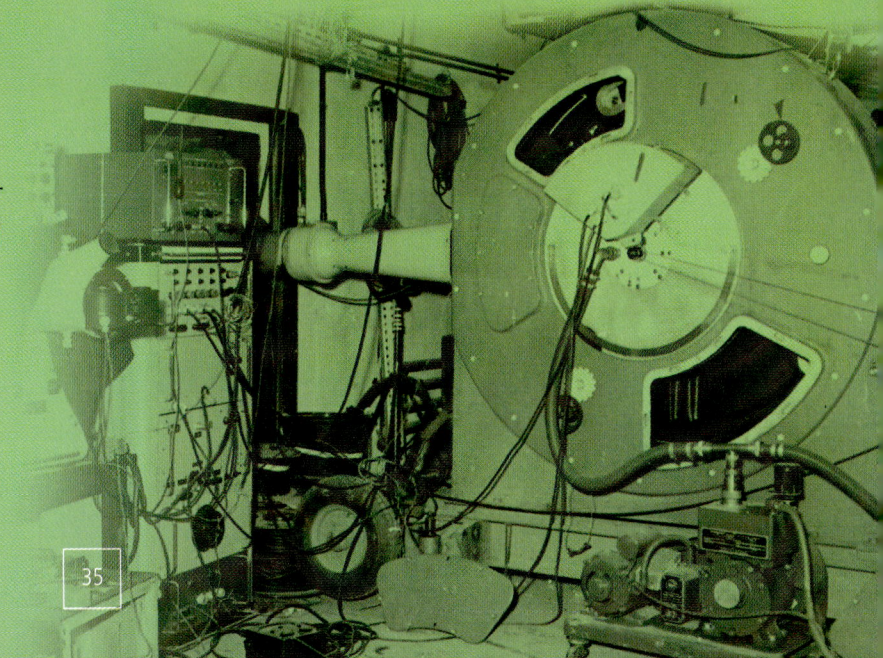

Testing TIMES

Until responding to international treaty obligations, the major nuclear weapons states, Britain included, have verified their warhead designs by live testing. Although the resources devoted to the programme were much less in Britain than in the USA or USSR, the ingenuity and dedication of Aldermaston's scientists and engineers kept Britain on a par with them in terms of technical achievement:

From A-bomb decision to deliverable test:	
USA	3 years
USSR	4 years
UK	5 years
France	5 years

From H-bomb decision to deliverable test:	
USA	6 years
USSR	7 years
UK	4 years
France	6 years

H-bomb in-service dates:	
USA	1956
USSR	1957
UK	1960
France	1972

Numbers of tests conducted: (APPROX.)	
USA	940
USSR	720
UK	45
France	210

Source: P.G.E.F. Jones

KEEPING THE PEACE •
The Aldermaston Story

Going
THERMONUCLEAR

Chapter 6

Going Thermonuclear

In July 1954, less than two years after the first test, the British Government took the decision to produce the 'hydrogen bomb', having become aware of its awesome destructive power from American tests. In simple terms, the modern hydrogen bomb has two stages, the 'primary' and the 'secondary'. The primary is effectively an atom bomb - a core of fissile material surrounded by high explosive which when detonated, compresses the core to a critical mass; at this point the fissile mass is flooded with neutrons which ensure a chain reaction. The energy from this explosion flows to the secondary, which comprises fissile material and thermonuclear 'fuel', such as lithium deuteride, heating and compressing it to produce both fission and fusion reactions.

However, this was by no means clear to Aldermaston's scientists in the 1950s; many ideas took shape as experimental devices which were tested in quick succession in the three years to 1958 before the optimum design was achieved.

◀ The crew of HMS *Narvik* observe the *Mosaic G1* shot from a safe distance on 16th May 1956.

The *Mosaic* test, conducted on the Monte Bello islands in 1956 was the first step on the road to a thermonuclear device and was designed to investigate the thermonuclear reactions of the light elements tritium and deuterium.

The culmination of Britain's atmospheric test programme was the *Grapple* series of trials at Malden Island and Christmas Island in the Pacific which took Britain into the thermonuclear era. The broad aim of the tests was to achieve the aim of a one megaton yield from a one ton warhead. A range of designs was tested on this series: a new concept of boosting the yield using solid thermonuclear 'fuel' and an external neutron source was first successfully tested with the development device known as *Orange Herald*.

The first two-stage design to be tested was *Short Granite*; on 15 May 1957, it was dropped from a Valiant bomber. But, at 300 kilotons, the yield was far short of the one megaton target. The problem was that a lack of computing power was limiting the designers' ability to predict the performance of the device, making intuition and guess-work an inevitable part of the process. Nevertheless the shot was regarded by the designers as a successful proof of principle.

Help was on hand with the acquisition of Aldermaston's first computers. Ferranti and English Electric machines installed in 1955 and 1956 were not powerful enough, but an IBM 704, installed early in 1957, successfully evaluated alternative designs for the secondary, due to be tested at a further series of trials, known as *Grapple-X*.

The *Grapple-X* device was a great success. Fired on 8 November 1957 off the southwest coast of Christmas Island, it yielded 1.8 megatons. For the next trial - *Grapple-Y* - a single warhead would be tested. The aim was a multimegaton yield more dependent on fusion than previous designs. *Grapple-Y* was dropped on 28 April 1958 giving 3 megatons. Even though the relative closeness of ground zero to the installations on Christmas Island meant deliberately limiting the yield, it was the largest ever British test.

Four months later, the final Christmas Island trial began. Code-named *Grapple-Z*, it tested a number of experimental designs, two of which were suspended from balloons, whilst the others in the series were freefall air drops. *Grapple-Z* culminated with a hollow gas-boosted device which

▼ Preparing a trials device during the *Grapple* series of atmospheric tests in 1958.

was fired on 23 September with a yield in the kiloton range. It was the United Kingdom's final atmospheric test.

Grapple had demonstrated that Aldermaston's weapon scientists had independently solved the essential problems of fission devices, staged weapons and boosting. But, although the staged devices had been dropped from aircraft, they were far from meeting the stringent safety and reliability

Chapter 6

◀ The classic shape of the mushroom cloud rises above Christmas Island, following the *Grapple-Y* test on 28 April 1958. With a yield of 3 megatons, it was Britain's biggest nuclear explosion.

KEEPING THE PEACE • The Aldermaston story

standards required for service use. Several more years of development and tests would have been needed, and indeed further trials, *Grapple-M* and *Grapple-O*, were in the planning stages.

Mounting the *Grapple* series of tests involved a massive logistics exercise; thousands of tons of supplies had to be transported to an inhospitable atoll on the other side of the world and a military Task Force of four thousand men fed and watered there for many months. The Army constructed base and airfield facilities and maintained repair workshops on Christmas and Malden Islands, while the Royal Navy transported the supplies as well as policing the waters around the test areas. Crucial to the success of the tests was the Royal Air Force; not only did they drop most of the trial devices, they collected meteorological and scientific data and supported the Royal Navy in maritime reconnaissance.

The atmospheric tests, conducted over just six years, propelled many young scientists and engineers at AWRE into some of the most innovative and exciting years of their lives. Separated from their families by thousands of miles for months on end, they worked in far-flung places to impossibly

Sketched in his spare time by a member of AWRE's scientific team, this design summed up his vision of life away from home: a palm tree on a tropical island, a grappling hook symbolic of the *Grapple* series, and dominating the scene, the familiar mushroom cloud of a nuclear explosion.

Chapter 6

tight timescales, all under a cloak of secrecy. With the Service personnel who supported the trials, they made a formidable team, whose enthusiasm for the new technology and the challenges of making it work thousands of miles from Aldermaston, forged links which survive today.

Some indication of the intensity of Aldermaston's work during the 1950s and early sixties is given by the fact that in addition to designing, manufacturing and testing full-scale nuclear devices, a whole series of so-called 'minor trials' was carried out in Australia over a ten year period - from 1953 to 1958 at Emu Field and from then to 1963 at Maralinga. *Kittens*, *Rats* and *Tims* were weapon development experiments and tests of components, particularly detonators, explosives and materials. The *Vixen* trials were safety related and in particular looked at the effects of the dispersion of nuclear materials in the event of a nuclear weapon being involved in a fire. In all, 550 minor trials had been carried out by April 1963. By that time, the Australian Government was becoming increasingly concerned about the use of Maralinga; and the availability of the Nevada Test Site for underground testing from 1962 made the case for its continuing use less valid. No further trials were conducted and in 1967, following a clean up operation, the Maralinga Range was finally given up.

The launching of Sputnik 1 by the USSR on 4 October 1957, a month before *Grapple-X*, had given the United Kingdom an opportunity to propose renewed collaboration on nuclear weapons with the United States. Since the McMahon Act of 1946 there had been few exchanges on nuclear matters and they had excluded weapon design. The Fuchs spy scandal in 1950 had not helped matters. The American attitude at the time was perhaps summed up by William Laurence writing in the New York Times immediately after Fuchs' arrest about a meeting three years before: *'And there in our midst stood Klaus Fuchs. There he was, this spy, standing right in the center of what we believed at the time to be the world's greatest secret'.*

Ironically, Sputnik offered a way forward: to offset this latest demonstration of Soviet power, Prime Minister Harold Macmillan suggested to President Eisenhower that *'the two countries... could go further towards pooling... efforts ... in such things as nuclear weapons'.* Eisenhower hinted that the McMahon Act might be amended to allow more collaboration. British scientists were invited to present some of their work to their American counterparts, who were impressed with the novelty of their designs.

Change was in the air. The 1958 moratorium on atmospheric testing and the closer collaboration with America permitted by an amended Atomic Energy Act focused attention on access to the existing fully tested and engineered American designs as a way of avoiding further nuclear trials.

Sunset at Christmas Island captured by one of AWRE's photographers during the *Grapple* series of trials in 1958.
Picture: Ted Baker

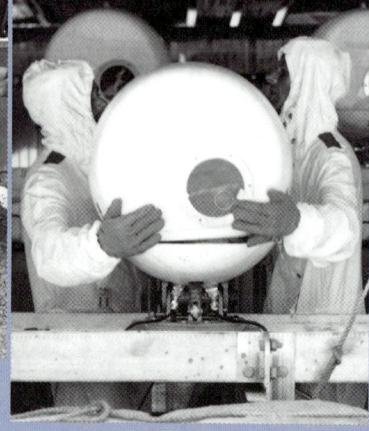

Chapter 6

After each shot, samples and records had to be recovered. Here, AWRE photographic staff prepare to collect film records on Malden Island during the first *Grapple* trial in 1957.

The certificate issued to all personnel who completed the jackstay transfer from the operational control ship HMS *Warrior* to the shore.

Spartan living accommodation for AWRE staff on Malden Island during the *Grapple* trials. The single light bulb attracts hundreds of moths as the occupant 'dresses for dinner'.

Malden Island camp, pictured in 1957. The mess tent is in the foreground, with accommodation for AWRE's scientific and technical staff beyond.

Gilbert and Ellice Islanders in traditional dress as part of the events arranged during the visit of HRH The Duke of Edinburgh to Port London in 1958

KEEPING THE PEACE • The Aldermaston Story

Lasting
PARTNERSHIPS

Chapter 7

Lasting Partnerships

On 2 July 1958, President Eisenhower signed amendments to the 1954 US Atomic Energy Act which opened the way to a bilateral agreement between Britain and America on nuclear weapon design information.

The turning point had come in October 1956, ironically with a disagreement, when America had refused to support the stance of Britain, France and Israel over the Suez crisis. To compensate Britain for the international political embarrassment suffered, by 1957 Eisenhower was increasingly determined to improve nuclear relations with Britain. In August of that year, the Soviet Union resumed nuclear weapons testing, a direct and negative response to an American suggestion that the USA would suspend testing if the Soviets ceased production of fissionable material for weapons. And the launch of Sputnik later in 1957 lead to a radical reappraisal of the Soviets' technical capabilities. At the same time, Anglo-American discussions on nuclear propulsion units for submarines and for stationing ballistic missiles on British soil were also in danger of stalling. Now, with the Act amended, the inertia could be overcome.

◀ The 1958 UK/US Agreement has formed the cornerstone of co-operation between Aldermaston and the US nuclear weapons laboratories for more than forty years.

Hot on the heels of the amendment came the signing, on 3 July 1958, of the *Agreement for Co-operation on the Uses of Atomic Energy for Mutual Defence Purposes*. The Agreement permitted an exchange of classified information which effectively would allow British delivery systems to be fitted with warheads based on American designs, as well as to improve the technical capability of both parties to the agreement in the field of nuclear weapons. In July 1959, an important amendment to the 1958 Agreement came into force which extended co-operation by - inter alia - permitting Anglo-American purchases and exchanges of fissile and thermonuclear material.

The technical exchanges which followed have been a cornerstone of life for the British nuclear weapon community ever since. Based around a series of Joint Working Groups, each concentrating on a specific area of physics, engineering and materials science, Aldermaston's specialists have for more than forty years been able to exchange and develop ideas with their counterparts from the American Laboratories to the benefit of the nuclear weapons programme on both sides of the Atlantic.

An important benefit of the 1958 Agreement was access for Britain to the Nevada Test Site, which the

Americans had been using since 1951. Britain's first underground nuclear test (UGT) took place on 1 March 1962; a further four tests had been mounted in Nevada when, at the end of 1965, the British Government decided to suspend nuclear testing. This policy was maintained by successive Governments until the need to validate the *Chevaline* warhead design led to the resumption of underground testing in Nevada in 1974. A total of twenty tests were carried out between May of that year and 26 November 1991, when the final test - codenamed *Bristol* - took place.

Measuring the performance of the test device involved a team of more than two hundred physics, electronics and optics specialists from Aldermaston, who worked closely with staff from the US laboratories to mount and record the trials. The device, placed in a heavily shielded diagnostics 'rack', which could weigh up to 200 tons, was lowered into place thousands of feet below the desert surface and linked to recording trailers capable of monitoring events taking place in less than one nanosecond.

In 1998, the fortieth anniversary year of the Agreement, nearly 500 AWE personnel were involved in 200 visits to the US laboratories at

▼ Sir William Cook, (centre, with pipe) who had been Scientific Director for the *Grapple* trials was Chairman of the UK delegation which visited the US in 1958. He is pictured at the Sandia National Laboratory with members of the US delegation including Dr. Norris Bradbury, Director of the Los Alamos Laboratory and Dr. Edward Teller, Director of the Lawrence Livermore Laboratory. Picture: Sandia National Laboratory.

Los Alamos, Sandia and Livermore and other plants within the American nuclear weapons community. There were return visits by more than 400 American personnel to Aldermaston and Burghfield during the same period. An important contribution from AWE was its impartial participation in the United States' 'Dual Revalidation Initiative', which reviewed the status of the W76 warhead, employed on the US *Trident*. system

Chapter 7

Members of AWE's trials team pose in the Nevada Desert; behind them, preparations are underway for Britain's last underground nuclear test - *Bristol* - which was fired in November 1991. National pride is evident in the sign, which is an anagram of the trial name.

Picture : Lawerence Livermore National Laboratory

KEEPING THE PEACE • The Aldermaston story

Of course, the Aldermaston story is inseparable from that of Britain's nuclear weapons but designing, testing and assembling the warhead is only one aspect of that story. To be part of an effective weapons system, a warhead must be safe to handle and store, must be delivered accurately to its target and must operate as intended when it gets there.

Over the last half century many companies and Government agencies have been involved in designing and testing bomb cases, delivery systems, electronics, radar and arming fuzing and firing mechanisms. The Royal Aircraft Establishment at Farnborough co-ordinated much of the design work, the Royal Aircraft Establishment at Boscombe Down conducted flight trials, whilst support from British industry,

Hunting Engineering Ltd in particular, has contributed to the nuclear weapons programme for more than fifty years. To list all those who have participated would be a roll-call of the best of British business past and present.

Each underground test had its own logo, designed to be an interpretation of the trial name. Here, Brunel and the Clifton Suspension Bridge are clear references to famous aspects of the city of Bristol.

Chapter 7

▲ The equipment rack for Britain's last underground nuclear test - codenamed *Bristol* - is carefully lowered into place below the Nevada Test Site in November 1991. The test device is housed in the section with the red band, whilst the rest of the rack contains diagnostic equipment. Picture: LLNL

▶ Practical partnerships - Aldermaston's J.C. 'Charlie' Martin, a world leader in pulsed power, makes a point to American warhead designer Edward Teller. Teller called Martin his 'scientific son'.

▲ Every underground nuclear test produced huge amounts of data in the first moments of the explosion. Much of this was recorded using banks of oscilloscopes, each fitted with a camera, seen here in one of the diagnostics trailers. Picture: LLNL

▲ The Nevada Test Site seen from the top of the test tower. Miles of cables relay huge amounts of data from the device to the recording trailers. Here, preparations are underway for Britain's last underground nuclear test. Picture: LLNL

50

KEEPING THE PEACE • The Aldermaston Story

The early
WEAPONS

Chapter 8

The early weapons

Through the close partnership between government, research scientists and industry, Service requirements and theoretical concepts were transformed into operational nuclear weapons. We have seen that the 1950s was a decade of intense activity at Aldermaston; tests were being planned and mounted, new designs were being developed whilst an operational stockpile was being built up and supported.

▲ A dummy *Blue Danube* '10,000 pound' bomb leaves a Valiant bomber during flight trials.

◄ A Vulcan bomber with a *Blue Steel* missile in the bomb bay flies above Niagara Falls in the mid 1960s.

Britain's first operational nuclear weapon, *Blue Danube*, was based on the *Hurricane* trials device and was in service from 1953 to 1961. With a yield specified by the Chiefs of Staff of 10KT, *Blue Danube* weighed in at 10,000 pounds and could just squeeze into the bomb bays of the V bombers which carried it. To save space the tail fins were retracted whilst in the aircraft, only being erected as the bomb dropped away. The fissile material was not inserted into the warhead until just prior to the mission, using an in-flight loading system. This provided a measure of safety when the weapon was in transit. Flight tests of *Blue Danube* with an inert warhead were carried out at the Orfordness range in Suffolk, and elsewhere.

Its successor, *Yellow Sun Mk 1*, was a 7000 pound free fall weapon. *Yellow Sun* had a distinctive flat front, designed to slow the descent of the weapon, so allowing the safe departure of the bombers, but giving it a decidedly unaerodynamic appearance. It was the first to have a warhead in the megaton range, the design of which - known as *Green Grass* - had been tested on *Grapple*. It was in service with the RAF from 1959 to 1962. To ensure the safety of the warhead, the core was filled with some 133 thousand ball bearings, which would have prevented accidental detonation. They would have been released prior to operational use.

Pending delivery of the *Yellow Sun* bomb casing, a short-lived interim weapon called *Violet Club* (which used the *Green Grass* warhead in a *Blue Danube* weapon casing) was in service with the RAF for about twelve months in 1958/59. Just twelve were made and they were fitted to Vulcan aircraft only.

Yellow Sun Mk.2 was Britain's first service thermonuclear weapon; the signing of the 1958 Agreement with the USA gave Aldermaston's designers the opportunity to develop an American two-stage warhead design known as *W28*. This design matched the desire for a 'megaton for a ton' device, so was clearly much smaller than its predecessor. The AWRE version was codenamed *Red Snow* and fitted into the *Yellow Sun* casing with plenty of room to spare. *Mk. 2* saw service with the RAF from 1961 to 1972.

▲ A *Yellow Sun Mk.2* poses besides a Victor bomber during loading trials in 1962.

▼ A Royal Navy Buccaneer drops its inert *Red Beard* tactical nuclear weapon during a trial in 1965.

Chapter 8

In the late 1960s, a Royal Navy Buccaneer displays its full weapons array, at the Royal Naval Air Station, Lossiemouth. In the centre is the tactical nuclear weapon *Red Beard*.
Picture: Fleet Air Arm Museum, Yeovilton

The tactical weapon *Red Beard* had a single stage kiloton warhead which had been tested in the *Buffalo* series of trials at Maralinga in Australia, in 1956. Although the design concept was similar to the *Blue Danube* warhead, an innovative means of implosion meant that the overall size could be greatly reduced; *Red Beard* had an all-up weight of about 2000 pounds. It was in service with the Royal Navy and the Royal Air Force between 1961 and 1971.

Blue Steel was Britain's first service nuclear missile; launched from a V bomber, it was in effect an unmanned supersonic aircraft in its own right, capable of speeds above Mach 2 at an altitude of 80,000 feet. Development had begun as early as 1954 by A.V. Roe and Co., who set up a Weapon Research Department as a private venture. Like *Yellow Sun Mk. 2*, *Blue Steel* was fitted with the *Red Snow* megaton warhead and was in service from 1962 to 1969.

The author (L) with Professor John Allen stands in front of a *Blue Steel* missile, which is part of AWE's Historical Collection. John Allen designed the *Blue Steel* casing for A.V. Roe (later AVRO) at their Woodford factory in 1954.

Chapter 8

▲ A cutaway drawing of *Yellow Sun Mk.1*. The distinctive flat front of the casing was designed to slow the fall of the weapon.

Blue Danube - Britain's first nuclear weapon, being prepared for service. ▶

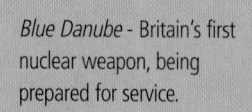

◀ The *Green Grass* warhead in the *Blue Danube* casing formed the interim weapon *Violet Club*. *Green Grass* was also deployed in *Yellow Sun Mk.1*

▲ The *Red Beard* tactical nuclear bomb tucked neatly into the bomb bay of a Buccaneer.

The outer casing of the *Red Snow* ▶ warhead, the UK version of the American *W28*, details of which were made available under the terms of the 1958 Agreement. *Red Snow* was fitted into *Blue Steel* and *Yellow Sun MK.2*

▼ *Blue Steel's* volatile mix of kerosene and high-test peroxide called for careful handling by the ground crew whilst refuelling.

56

KEEPING THE PEACE • The Aldermaston Story

WE 177 and beyond
NEW GENERATIONS OF WEAPONS

Chapter 9

WE 177 and beyond - **new generations of weapons**

In the late 1950s, the Chiefs of Staff had identified a need for a multi - purpose nuclear weapon which could be deployed with the low level attack aircraft TSR-2, then under development.

Despite the eventual cancellation of TSR-2, development of the bomb went ahead. Known simply as *WE 177*, it was lightweight and versatile - the first of a new generation.

At Aldermaston, warhead design was pursued with urgency. On 1 March 1962, 1200 feet below the Nevada Desert, the test device was successfully detonated in the first of Britain's underground nuclear tests, codenamed *Pampas*. Access to the Nevada Test Site was one of the benefits flowing from the 1958 Agreement.

Later that year, AWRE's warhead designers were able to advise their Director, Dr. N. Levin (William Penney having left in 1959) that such a weapon could be produced by 1966. The first *WE 177* (the thermonuclear Type B) was delivered to RAF Cottesmore in September of that year. A single stage version (Type A) was delivered to the Royal Navy in 1972. Over the following years a remarkable range of aircraft was fitted to carry the weapon. They included the Vulcan, Jaguar and Tornado and - in the Naval role - the Sea King, Scimitar, Buccaneer and Sea Harrier. By the time of its final withdrawal in 1998, *WE 177* had been in service longer than any other British nuclear weapon.

The Royal Air Force was not destined to have the monopoly of nuclear capability for long: in the early 1950s strategists had considered that a nuclear weapon might be delivered by sea, perhaps smuggled into a British harbour in the hold of a ship. A decade later, delivery from beneath the sea by means of submarine launched ballistic missiles offered a new way forward. The cancellation of the joint US/UK missile project - *Skybolt* - led to the 1962 Nassau agreement, by which the Americans agreed to provide Britain with details of their submarine launched missile system - *Polaris*.

This posed a challenge for Aldermaston's warhead designers; the need to sit three warheads atop a missile only fifty-four inches in diameter called for a smaller warhead than anything previously designed. At this time, the UK had not achieved the level of computer-based modelling and

◀ A Royal Navy *Trident D-5* missile on a test firing. Each *Vanguard* class submarine is capable of carrying sixteen missiles.

simulation capability which existed in the US; but the *A3 Polaris* missile was ready for flight, increasing the pressure on AWRE to produce a viable design.

Aldermaston's warhead designers solved the problem by scaling down the first stage of the existing *WE 177* (the primary) to match the size and mass required to fit it in the *Polaris* re-entry body. AWRE completed its test programme in 1965 and in 1968 the first of the Polaris submarines - HMS *Resolution* - went on patrol, armed with sixteen missiles, each capable of carrying three warheads in the kiloton range.

By the mid 1960s, the Government had concluded that the *Polaris* system was at risk from Soviet improvements in anti-ballistic missile defences. The Americans responded with a new system - *Poseidon* - but in Britain a decision was taken in 1972 to improve the ability of *Polaris* to penetrate these defences. In this way was born the uniquely British system known as *Chevaline*. AWRE's scientists and engineers, together with those at RAE Farnborough, Hunting Engineering and many other British companies devised a sophisticated system of decoys and disguises as well as a redesigned warhead which was 'hardened' against nuclear

◀ A test firing of a Royal Navy *Polaris A3* missile. *Polaris* and its successor *Chevaline*, were in service from 1968 to 1996.

attack. The so-called 'Improved Front End', which was capable of manoeuvring in space to deploy its warheads and decoys, was fitted to the existing *Polaris* missiles and was in service from 1980 to 1996. It was a tribute to the skill and ingenuity of the many hundreds of specialist staff involved.

The Government had started thinking about a long term successor for its *Polaris* submarines as early as 1977 and in 1980 a decision was announced that Britain was to acquire the *Trident* system.

Launched from the larger Vanguard - class submarines, Trident is a multiple independently targeted re-entry vehicle system - MIRV. Each operational submarine carries up to sixteen *Trident*

Chapter 9

The *WE 177* free-fall nuclear bomb, slung from the wing pylon of a Sea Harrier, pictured in 1988. *WE 177* was a versatile weapon capable of operating in a strategic and tactical role. It was in service for a total of 32 years.

D-5 missiles; as a result of the 1998 Strategic Defence Review, each boat now carries a total of forty-eight warheads.

Although the *Trident* delivery system is American, with the missiles being supplied by Lockheed Martin, the design, manufacture and testing of the UK's warhead was the responsibility of AWE's scientists and engineers who incorporated in the British version the results of research carried out during the late 1970s. Development trials of the UK's *Trident* warhead design were conducted at the Nevada Test site between 1984 and 1986. In 1994 the first *Trident* boat, HMS *Vanguard*, entered service with the Royal Navy.

But by then the world order was changing. With the end of the Cold War, governments across the world were reviewing their strategic defences. It was in this context that the Naval variant of *WE 177* was taken out of service in 1992 and in April 1995 the British government announced that *WE 177* was to be totally withdrawn. A few short weeks after its election in May 1997, the Labour government declared that the withdrawal date was being brought forward as an indication of its commitment to reducing the global nuclear stockpile.

On 31 March 1998, the last *WE 177* was withdrawn from RAF Marham; for the first time in forty-five years, the RAF had no nuclear capability. AWE's assembly facilities at Burghfield were already busy with dismantling the warheads and on 21 August 1998, several weeks ahead of schedule, the painstaking breakdown of the very last one was completed. As the twentieth century drew to a close, a major operational task for AWE was dismantling the *Chevaline* warheads, achieving a target of one third of the stockpile broken down by the end of 1999.

Trident is now Britain's sole nuclear weapon; with high accuracy targeting and an option of two warhead yields, it can operate in both strategic and sub-strategic roles. It remains AWE's principal task to meet the requirements of the Ministry of Defence to maintain the *Trident* warhead safely and reliably in service, to time and to cost.

The decommissioning team at AWE Burghfield with the last *WE 177* to be broken down, pictured in 1998.

Chapter 9

▼ The *Chevaline* 'Improved Front End' comprised two re-entry bodies and a wide range of decoys, collectively called 'penetration aids'. The Penetration Aids Carrier (PAC) is seen here mounted on the second stage of a *Polaris* missile.

▲ Each *Chevaline* warhead was contained in a re-entry body (ReB) made of a special material designed to protect it from the heat of re-entry into the atmosphere as well as from nuclear attack. In this 1979 picture, the shape of the ReB is being measured using a gauge array at ROF Burghfield.

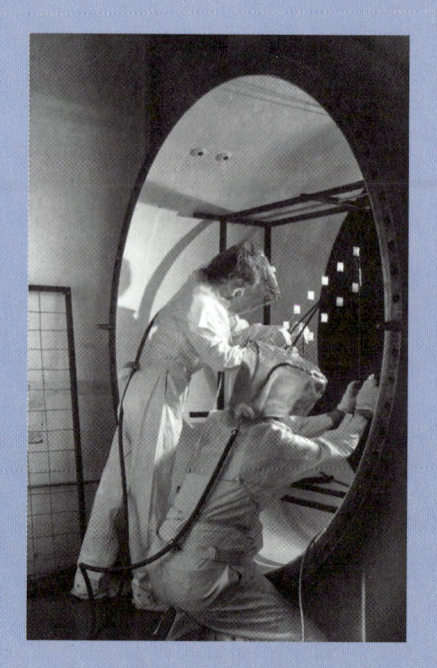

▲ *Chevaline* warheads were 'disguised' against counter attack by ballistic missiles. In this 1979 picture, part of the disguise mechanism is being tested in a vacuum chamber called *Gollum*, located in building N51 at Aldermaston. The air hoods are to protect the scientists from lead dust generated by the trial.

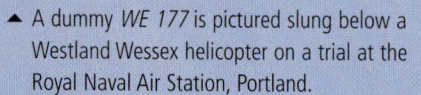

▲ *WE 177* was a parachute retarded bomb; a test vehicle is seen here on completion of a flight trial at the West Freugh range in August 1970.

▲ A dummy *WE 177* is pictured slung below a Westland Wessex helicopter on a trial at the Royal Naval Air Station, Portland.

KEEPING THE PEACE • The Aldermaston Story

Prohibited
PLACES

GOVERNMENT·PROPERTY

PERSONS·CAUSING·WILFUL·DAMAGE

WILL·BE·PROSECUTED

Chapter 10

Prohibited Places

Although it is the name 'Aldermaston' which has become synonymous with Britain's nuclear programme, it is only one of many sites which have been associated with it during the last five decades. Such was the secrecy surrounding the atomic weapons programme that the involvement of a variety of Government establishments was not widely known; indeed some of the sites, including Aldermaston, quietly disappeared from the maps, which continued to show woods, meadows and footpaths long since replaced by workshops and laboratories.

It was in the library at Woolwich Arsenal (an outstation of Fort Halstead) in June 1947 that William Penney, as Chief Superintendent Armament Research, held the first meeting with the thirty-four scientists and engineers who were to form the core of his team. This was in effect the inauguration of the Basic High Explosives Research Division (usually referred to as HER) which started work later that year at Fort Halstead in Kent, a site which owed its origins to the Napoleonic wars. The development of the detonators, and arming, fuzing and firing units for *Blue Danube* continued at Fort Halstead until 1956. At Woolwich

◀ A rough and ready sign outside 'A' building at Woolwich Common carried a stern warning to potential vandals in 1956.

Arsenal (for high explosives) and Woolwich Common (for weapon electronics production), work in support of the nuclear weapon programme also continued into the 1950s. An environmental testing facility at Woolwich Common was used throughout the 1960s before being transferred to Aldermaston.

Trials using conventional explosives were undertaken at a remote site in Essex: Foulness in the Thames Estuary. Foulness had supported the nuclear weapons programme since 1947. With its associated ranges at Havengore Island and Potton Island, it played an important part in support of the atmospheric tests, as well as conducting research into the effects of blast on structures. Indeed, it was at Foulness that the first test device, without its fissile components, was assembled in the spring and summer of 1952. A wide range of test facilities allowed experiments on air blast, underwater shock, vibration and climatic effects. Foulness survived as an AWE site until 1997, when its management passed to the adjacent Army range at Shoeburyness. It still remains available to support the nuclear weapons programme and in 1998 AWE carried out a series of high explosives trials there.

Blacknest is a former country house two miles west of Aldermaston; at the centre of a network of seismic monitoring stations, it plays an important part in the international verification of the ban on nuclear testing. From 1958, Blacknest's forensic seismologists contributed much to the success of the long running negotiations in Geneva which led to the Partial Test Ban Treaty of 1964 and eventually to the Comprehensive Test Ban Treaty more than thirty years later.

Amongst the pioneering work carried out by AWRE was a series of experiments known as Operation *Orpheus*; conducted initially at Foulness and later at the Greenside Mine in Cumbria and the Excelsior Tunnel at Kit Hill in Cornwall they tested the theory that underground nuclear tests could be disguised by 'decoupling' them from the surrounding rocks. The results of this work, carried out between 1959 and 1962, provided valuable data to assist AWRE in the detection of nuclear tests. Development of linear cross arrays of seismometers lowered the detection threshold for seismic events; because they were capable of being focussed on a point anywhere in the world, they enabled AWRE to estimate the location of the signal source. Four such arrays were deployed, in Australia, Canada, India and Eskdalemuir in Scotland.

In 1954, AWRE took over a Royal Aircraft Establishment range on the windswept coast of East Anglia, at Orford Ness. Here, an impressive

▼ Now a National Trust property, the shingle ridge of Orford Ness is dominated by the slowly decaying 'pagodas' which were built by AWRE as environmental test laboratories in the 1950s
Picture: National Trust Photographic Library/Joe Cornish

environmental testing facility was developed, characterised by the distinctive blast-proof 'pagodas'. It was here that ballistic trials of the *Blue Danube* bomb casing had been carried out and *WE 177's* ability to withstand 'lay down' was tested on the rocket sledge. Reducing demand for its facilities led to closure in 1971, with much of the environmental testing equipment, including a centrifuge, being transferred to Aldermaston. This device, with a radius of four metres, can generate forces of more than 200g and is still in use today.

Orford Ness is now owned by the National Trust. It is a place of shingle ridges and huge skies, where the gently decaying buildings are silent reminders of the special part they played in Britain's military history.

Two Royal Ordnance Factories, at Cardiff in South Wales and Burghfield, about six miles from Aldermaston, have long been associated with the nuclear programme. In 1954, the former ammunition factory at Burghfield was converted to support Aldermaston's work, particularly in the field of high explosives. Later, purpose built warhead assembly facilities were constructed, the first two in 1960, with two more becoming operational in 1990. Special safety features led to these unusual buildings being nicknamed 'Gravel Gerties'. Burghfield continues to play a significant part in Britain's nuclear programme and during the late 1990s has made an important contribution to nuclear disarmament with the majority of its assembly facilities being dedicated to dismantling *WE 177* and *Chevaline* warheads.

The Cardiff factory, now surrounded by modern commercial development and suburban housing, started life in 1940 with the manufacture of 25-pounder field guns and after the war made a wide range of goods for the civilian market; mining plant, printing presses and concrete components for the post war house-building programme. Cardiff had its first taste of the nuclear age at the end of the 1950s when it was required to manufacture graphite for the Atomic Energy Research Establishment at Harwell ; by 1960, when advancing warhead design demanded special components, Cardiff's close association with the nuclear weapons programme began.

The factory specialized in the manufacture of components from depleted uranium and beryllium, a strange metal only one quarter of the density of steel, yet with great strength, resistance to high temperatures and capable of being machined to very fine tolerances. AWE Cardiff moved to the forefront of beryllium engineering; not only were weapons parts made here, beryllium's transparency to x-rays has been of benefit to medical science. Almost everyone in Britain who has been x-rayed has been examined through a window of Cardiff beryllium. With the end of the *Trident* production programme in sight, reduced demand for the factory's unique skills led to its closure in 1997.

◀ The vacuum induction hot press at AWE Cardiff, used since the 1960s to produce beryllium components, including those required for the *Trident* warhead.

Chapter 10

AWE's Foulness site was used mainly to study blast effects, using conventional explosives. Here, an underwater shock and blast trial is being conducted in the 40-metre pond.

Chapter 10

Field gun manufacture began at ROF Cardiff in 1940. At the peak, 1,700 guns per month were being produced. Here, 25 pounder gun barrels are coming off the production line.

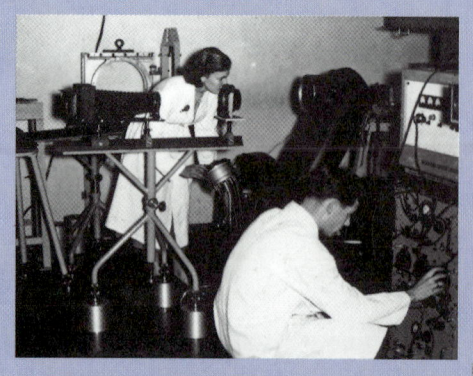

The shock tube at Fort Halstead being used to investigate the propagation of a stimulated nuclear blast on a model of a building, in the early 1950s.

The distinctive roofs of the new assembly buildings at ROF Burghfield, photographed as they neared completion in February 1960. In the top centre of the picture can be seen part of the factory's railway network, which was connected to the main line for the transport of wartime munitions. Workers also travelled to the site by special trains from Reading.

To test the 'decoupling' theory, more than 3000 pounds of high explosive were detonated in a disused lead mine at Greenside in the Lake District. Here, the AWRE scientist in charge of the operation, Edward Drake-Seager, is seen in the flooded 175 fathom level of the mine, shortly after the explosion on 15 December 1959. The canary in a cage was the traditional miners' way of detecting dangerous gas.

Part of Operation *Orpheus* took place in the Excelsior Tunnel - a disused tin mine near Callington, Cornwall. Small charges were fired in a six foot cavity some three hundred feet below ground. Here, AWRE staff are entering the tunnel, wearing breathing apparatus as a precaution against toxic gas.

Blacknest Lodge, a few miles from Aldermaston, is the home of AWE's forensic seismology group. AWE scientists have made important contributions to international test ban treaty negotiations and in developing verification techniques.

Campaigning DAYS

No one would deny that nuclear weapons can arouse strong emotions. Those opposed to them found their voice in the Campaign for Nuclear Disarmament - CND - which was established in 1958. CND organized a series of marches from Aldermaston to London, which for a few years attracted huge crowds, with more than 10,000 people marching in 1959 and 1960. In the latter year, the number of marchers had swollen tenfold by the time of the final rally in Trafalgar Square. Although Aldermaston continues to attract the attention of anti-nuclear campaigners, by the 1980s, the protestors could be numbered in their tens rather than their thousands.

Taking no CHANCES

Inevitably, Aldermaston handles some of the most dangerous substances known to science and does so in a safe and responsible way. But it is equally responsible to be able to react effectively to an emergency should it arise.

By the mid 1950s, Aldermaston had a limited capability to field a three-ton Bedford truck and a set of basic equipment capable of responding to incidents on site as well as to an off-site accident involving a nuclear weapon. The capability developed rapidly with a range of radiation detection monitors designed and built at Aldermaston enabling AWRE to set up an environmental monitoring programme.

As the range of equipment expanded, so did the vehicle fleet; the original Bedford truck was replaced with specialist trucks and trailers equipped as mobile command centres. Arrangements were made with the Royal Air Force to transport vehicles and equipment, so providing a worldwide response capability.

The first vehicle-based mobile command and control unit came into service in 1960; it also contained a Health Physics Laboratory and was in service for more than twenty years, being replaced by a larger Emergency Response Vehicle and trailer in the early 1980s.

Today, AWE's Emergency Response teams have a fleet of purpose built vehicles and specialist equipment and communications, capable of providing a rapid and flexible response to an emergency on or off the AWE sites. Support is provided to the Ministry of Defence in the event of an incident involving the transport of nuclear weapons or material. This capability is tested and refined on a regular basis with realistic field training exercises, usually in conjunction with County or District emergency planners, Police and other civil emergency services and the Armed Forces.

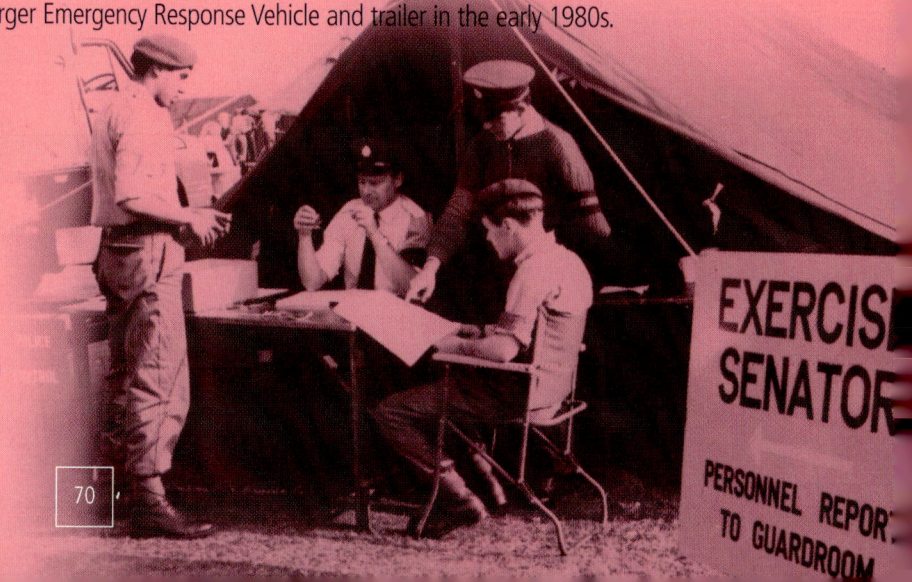

KEEPING THE PEACE • The Aldermaston Story

Swords into PLOUGHSHARES

Chapter 11

Swords into Ploughshares

By the mid 1960s a number of factors had led to overcapacity at Aldermaston. The *Blue Streak* and *Skybolt* missile systems had been cancelled and - with *WE 177* and *Polaris* soon to enter service - Britain voluntarily ceased underground testing between 1965 and 1974. This suspension of nuclear warhead development led to AWRE's embarking on a programme of research in non-nuclear areas. It was a time of great innovation.

Earlier, Aldermaston had become involved in the UKAEA's power reactor development programme, with work on fuel element manufacture beginning in 1960 . Its two objectives were to produce a specification for the Windscale fuel production plant for the Prototype Fast Reactor (later constructed at Dounreay) and to build a 'demonstration' plant on a scale suitable for production rates for a 600 MW PFR. By 1965, such a plant was operating successfully in building A50. However, when AWRE was transferred to the Ministry of Defence in 1973, Aldermaston's support to the power reactor programme ceased - and with it the fuel production work in A 50.

◀ AWE's impressive stand at the 'Tomorrow's World Live' exhibition in June 2000. The James Bond theme illustrated AWE's capability in the sphere of sophisticated security systems. The AWE stand was one of the most popular at the show.

The skills which Aldermaston had developed in the nuclear field were widely recognized as having applications elsewhere. Shortly after the start of the Concorde supersonic aircraft programme in 1962 it was realized that with its high cruising altitude of between fifty-five and sixty thousand feet, the aircraft would be subject to significant levels of cosmic radiation. Because of its experience in the field of radiation measurement and the development of associated instrumentation, AWRE was awarded a contract by the Ministry of Aviation to measure the radiation dose-equivalent rate at cruise altitudes and to develop solar flare warning instrumentation.

This work continued throughout the 1960s, with AWRE scientists working in collaboration with their French counterparts. An important part of the work was instrumented balloon flight trials, conducted at Aire-sur-Adour in France and at RAF Cardington, former home of the ill-fated airship, the R101. The in-flight radiation warning meter developed by AWRE is still in use in Concorde aircraft today. Aldermaston's expertise in the field of materials science also led to the development of carbon fibre disc brakes for Concorde.

Campaigning in the run up to the 1964 general election, Labour leader Harold Wilson pledged to create a modern industrial Britain forged in the 'white heat' of technology. An early manifestation of this was the creation by the newly elected Labour government of a Ministry of Technology (Mintech), with overall responsibility for government research bodies, including the UKAEA.

In 1965 the Science and Technology Act came into force, which permitted the UK Atomic Energy Authority to undertake *'scientific research in such matters not connected with atomic energy'*. The benefit of this legislation to AWRE was that the specialist teams which had been developed over many years and whose contribution to the nuclear weapons programme would doubtless be required in the years to come could be kept intact, whilst redundancies could be avoided.

Developments in bio-medical technology were one of the most important benefits of this initiative. Indeed, the development of nuclear weapons had equipped Aldermaston with a range of disciplines which lent themselves well to medical engineering: applied physics, nuclear physics, chemistry and chemical technology, metallurgy, and mathematics, supported by mechanical and electrical designers, precision engineering and high speed optical and electronic capabilities.

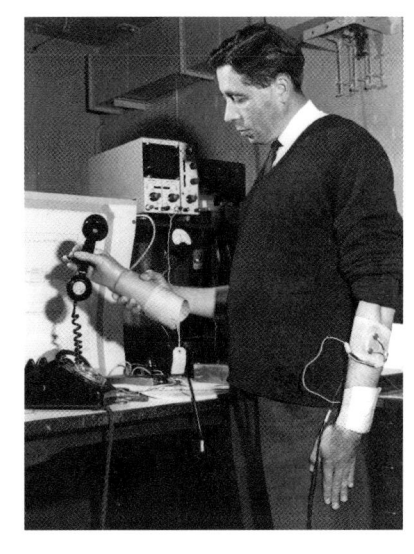

◀ An artificial hand, remotely controlled by myo-electric impulses from the user's muscles, seen here under test in 1967.

Most of the medical research was carried out under contract from the Ministry of Health. One task was to evaluate an electrically powered artificial hand which had been designed by a Russian doctor. The hand was controlled by myo-electric signals from the patient's remaining muscles, with electrodes being placed on the forearm. This relatively crude device was developed by AWRE into a sophisticated system incorporating advanced techniques for giving the artificial hand 'feel'. A difficult assignment was the development of an ankle joint for an artificial foot; to be comfortable to the patient, the prosthesis had to match the mechanical properties of the human ankle as closely as possible, in terms of resistance and degrees of movement. AWRE's expertise in materials led also to the development of a titanium alloy hip joint in conjunction with St. Bartholomew's Hospital.

Chapter 11

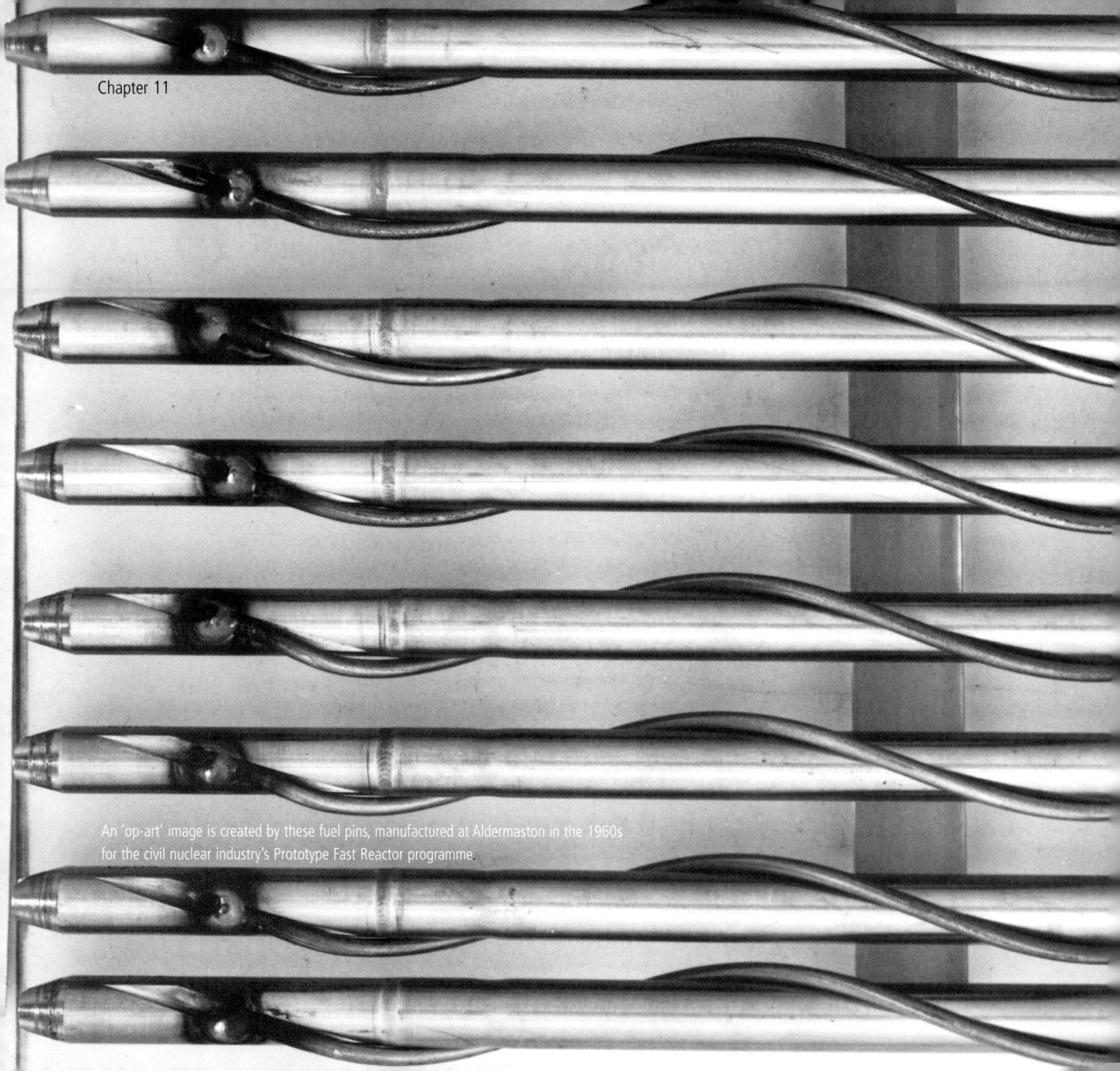

An 'op-art' image is created by these fuel pins, manufactured at Aldermaston in the 1960s for the civil nuclear industry's Prototype Fast Reactor programme.

Reports by Aldermaston's scientists on the effectiveness of existing thermal imaging equipment led to its much wider application, for example in the techniques which today are of such value in locating the victims of earthquakes or explosions. The scope of AWRE's involvement in a range of medical research projects broadened to include studies into the corrosion of medical implants, a flexible gastroscope using fibre optics, a laser scalpel manipulator, work with Guy's Hospital to develop an 'arterial drill' to clear blocked arteries, development of dental fillings and the evaluation of kidney dialysis machines.

At the peak of the programme in 1969, AWRE was collaborating with no fewer than twenty-seven hospitals and had filed seventeen patents. The barrier to expansion lay not with the technically sophisticated solutions offered by Aldermaston's scientists and engineers but with their cost, which effectively put them out of the reach of a tightly budgeted Health Service.

In other areas, too, AWRE was involved in pioneering research: the 'APACE' project, based at the Blacknest site was operated under contract to the Ministry of Technology to develop the application of computers to engineering. APACE was designed to provide industry with specialist training and to offer a consultancy service. Time on Aldermaston's mainframe computers was also available to industry. In this way, AWRE was at the forefront of many techniques which are now widely used such as numerical control of machine tools and computer aided design.

Technical discussions underway on AWRE's stand at the 'Cadex 69' ▶ exhibition. For a short time, the APACE programme at Blacknest was a leader in developing the application of computers to engineering.

Chapter 11

Training was offered in a technique devised at AWRE to apply method study to the design process; known as 'PABLA' (problem analysis by logical approach), it aimed at helping the designer to better meet the needs of the customer. Initially, APACE was a success with 526 people attending courses in 1968, but it never achieved its goal of financial self-sufficiency and by 1970 the largest group of students was from AWRE itself.

In other spheres, Aldermaston carried out research in a wide range of disciplines, including design and fatigue testing of bridges, strengthened building materials, heat resistant paints, tunnelling machines, pedestrian conveyors and multilayer thick films, which led to the miniaturization of electronic circuits. There was even an attempt to improve production methods for Marks and Spencer's range of women's lingerie. However, a recommendation that garments should be glued together rather than sewn was not taken up!

In 1966 Aldermaston beat off stiff competition to win a contract to supply massive fifty-ton multi-channel spectrographs to Pennsylvania and Yale Universities in America and a third to the Max Planck institute in Heidelberg. Understanding the nucleus of the atom had been fundamental to AWRE's early work and a multi channel spectrograph designed in-house was operational by 1960. It was this proven track record which led to Aldermaston's largest export order.

Aldermaston's products went even further into space than the instruments on Concorde: on 5 May 1967 Ariel III, the first all-British satellite was launched from NASA's Western Test Range in California. On board was a miniature high environment tape recorder manufactured at Aldermaston. Designed to run at extremes of temperature and pressure, the recorder successfully completed many hundreds of orbits.

For a while the site had the atmosphere of a university campus, but the demise of Mintech in 1970 and the transfer of AWRE to the Ministry of Defence in 1973, coupled with the growing demands of the nuclear weapons programme, particularly *Chevaline*, led to a reduction in other work. It was not to increase until the mid 1990s, when under the contractorized management arrangements, some further diversification work was undertaken.

With a reduction in the nuclear weapons programme, diversification was again seen as offering a number of advantages. According to a strategy document issued in 1995, it would attract and motivate good quality staff, exploit many of AWE's skills and facilities and ensure the full use of under-utilized resources. By doing so, it was hoped that the old image of AWE as the 'bomb factory' would be transformed.

In the years that followed AWE refined its approach to concentrate on a number of specialist areas. Among the ideas which made good progress were:

- A hand-held alpha/beta radiation monitor. This unique design is intrinsically safe so can be used in areas containing explosives or flammable materials. During 1999 it was being prepared for production and sale under licence.

- 'Customized' molecules of compounds called 'calixarenes'. By modifying the molecules of these compounds, AWE's scientists are now able to capture selected heavy metals from waste streams. The development could play an important part in cleaning up polluted water supplies or recovering precious metals.

- An ingenious process developed at Aldermaston allows the cheap and accurate shaping of boron carbide - the third hardest substance known to science. Commercial applications in personal protection and materials grinding (of interest to the pharmaceutical industry for example) are being explored.

A replica of one of the famous 'Lewis' chess pieces made from boron carbide, the third hardest material known to science. Techniques developed at Aldermaston permit unprecedented levels of detail to be achieved.

- In the field of medical science, where AWRE had many successes in the 1960s, scale replicas of bone structures, produced as a result of AWE's applied technology, were successfully used to assist a surgeon in operations in a local hospital.

But it should not be forgotten that Aldermaston's principal role has always been and surely will continue to be, to support the UK's nuclear weapons programme. Throughout the diversification programmes of the 1960s, 70s and 90s, support for the nation's nuclear stockpile and the maintenance of capability was at the forefront of Aldermaston's priorities.

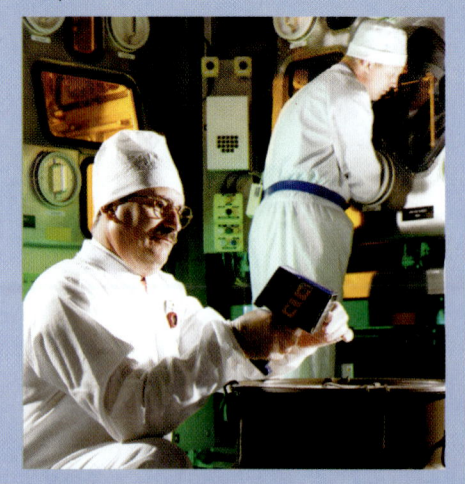

Chapter 11

▲ Testing a hand held radiation monitor, designed at Aldermaston to be safe for use in hazardous areas. A prototype was demonstrated at the Royal Navy and British Army Equipment Exhibition at Farnborough in 1997.

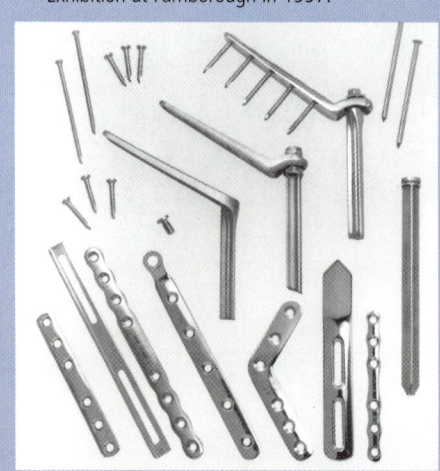

▼ An inspector from AWRE carries out a vacuum test of a multi-channel spectrograph designed at Aldermaston for Yale University. It was one of three such machines shipped to overseas institutions in 1966.

▼ A prototype steerable infra-red surgical cutter using a helium/neon laser, designed at AWRE in 1968.

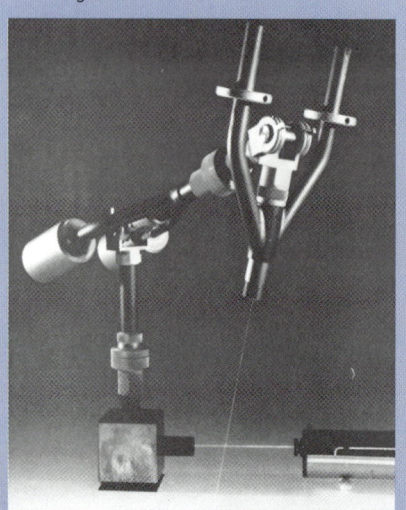

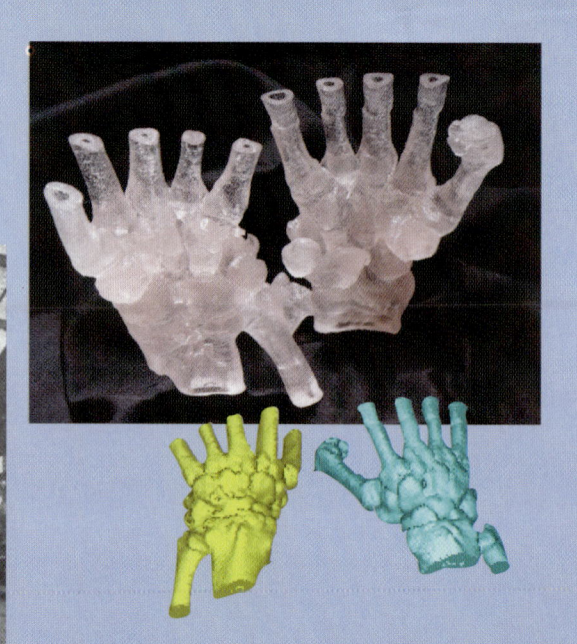

▲ Aldermaston's expertise in multi-axis x-radiography and computer aided design have been combined to produce three dimensional models of bone fractures, which will assist surgeons to plan every stage of complex operations.

▲ During the 1960s, AWRE carried out research into corrosion of medical implants, with the aim of extending their life and advising surgeons on the most suitable materials. This is a selection of screws, nails and plates included in the study.

▲ Part of the equipment used at Aldermaston in the 1960s for the manufacture of nuclear fuel elements for the civil power industry.

KEEPING THE PEACE • The Aldermaston Story

Winds of
CHANGE

Chapter 12

Winds of Change

Aldermaston has witnessed many changes since gliders took off from the airfield in the 1940s. As well as developments on the ground with the construction of new facilities, in the fields of organization, business and infrastructure, another thread of change has run through the Aldermaston story.

Following the closure of Aldermaston airfield, which was under the control of the Ministry of Civil Aviation, the Ministry of Supply assumed responsibility for the site, with construction being managed by the Ministry of Works. Management of the site passed from the Ministry of Supply to the Weapons Group of the United Kingdom Atomic Energy Authority in 1954. In 1965, UKAEA was placed under the newly-created Ministry of Technology and in 1973, the Ministry of Defence assumed responsibility under the terms of the Atomic Energy Authority (Weapons Group) Act, 1973.

The Royal Ordnance Factories which supported the nuclear programme - Burghfield and Cardiff - alone of the ROFs were transferred from the Ministry of Supply to the Ministry of Aviation in

◀ The corporate flags of Hunting-BRAE Ltd (operator of AWE from 1993 to 2000) and AWE Management Ltd, who took over the management contract from 1 April 2000.

1959, in recognition of their special role. (The others went to the Army Department of the Ministry of Defence). Later, Burghfield and Cardiff were absorbed into the Ministry of Technology and subsequently became part of the Procurement Executive of the Ministry of Defence.

In 1987, the two nuclear Ordnance Factories were placed under the direct management of Aldermaston. To reflect the creation of a single nuclear weapons industry for the United Kingdom, with research and production under a single management, the name was changed to the Atomic Weapons Establishment - AWE.

Further change was in the offing. By the late 1980s, the area around Aldermaston had developed radically from the rural backwater it had been in the 1950s. The expansion of Basingstoke as a major commercial centre and the spread of high-tech companies along the Thames and Kennet valleys towards Newbury had forced up wages and created a real shortage of skilled employees. In its Report for 1988/89, the Commons Defence Select Committee raised concerns that this shortage of staff might have implications for the production of *Trident* warheads. In the wake of this, the Prime Minister, Margaret Thatcher, asked Sir Francis Tombs, Chairman of Rolls Royce, to examine the role and organization of AWE.

Tombs visited AWE during July 1989 and recommended 'contractorization' as the optimum solution to the *Trident* production problems. In a statement to the Commons on 5 December 1989, Secretary of State for Defence, Tom King, announced that the need for increased *Trident* production from 1992, against a background of skill shortages, posed an increasing challenge and one which required greater production management capability. He added that the Government's view was that the best way to achieve this goal was by full contractorization; the Government Owned, Contractor Operated concept - GOCO - had operated successfully in the US nuclear weapons laboratories for forty years, he said.

A small number of commercial managers would join AWE in 1990 following competitive tendering, whilst legislation would be introduced to allow full contractorization as soon as possible. The AWE Act duly received the Royal Assent on 20 July 1991, paving the way for the next major change. So it was that on 1 April 1993 AWE began its new regime of commercial management. Hunting-BRAE Ltd were awarded the first seven year management contract

▼ The Hunting-BRAE flag is raised for the first time outside Aldermaston's main administrative building, F6.1, on 1 April 1993.

as the result of a competitive tendering exercise. Hunting-BRAE Ltd was a joint venture company comprising Hunting Engineering (whose connection with the UK nuclear weapons programme began in the late 1940s), Brown and Root, and AEA Technology, whose predecessor, UKAEA, had managed AWRE from 1954 to 1973. AWE's 6,000 strong workforce transferred from the Civil Service to a new employing company, AWE Plc, and the Ministry of Defence established a Compliance Office at Aldermaston to ensure that the new managing contractor met its obligations under the contract.

Chapter 12

In this aerial view of AWRE taken in 1953, the outline of the wartime airfield can be clearly seen. The explosives area (L) and fissile material processing buildings (centre) are already in place, but much of the site remains undeveloped. Aircraft parking bays (bottom R) have not yet been removed, whilst the first of the Tadley housing estates is visible (centre R).

KEEPING THE PEACE • The Aldermaston story

Commercial management brought with it many changes in the conduct of business at AWE, with the introduction of modern financial, project management and business planning systems. Crucial to this was the achievement of industry standard quality registration ISO 9001 in 1993. In June of that year, the Defence Secretary, Malcolm Rifkind, visited Aldermaston to present the certificate, in recognition that AWE's quality management systems met the required standards of design, development and production of Defence products. It was one of the first examples of the major change in philosophy which contractorization had brought.

During the seven year period of the contract, a major rationalization of site facilities was begun; modern facilities replaced some of those which had seen service for more than forty years. And by the end of 1999 AWE's workforce had been reduced to about 4,500.

During 1999, the Ministry of Defence sought tenders from industry for a contract to operate AWE for the next ten years; perhaps surprisingly, Hunting-BRAE as the 'sitting tenants' did not win the contract. On 1 April 2000, a day which also marked the fiftieth anniversary of Aldermaston's first association with the nuclear defence programme, AWE Management Ltd raised its flag outside the main administration block. AWEML is an equal partnership of three companies with long track records in the management of complex defence facilities and of nuclear programmes: British Nuclear Fuels Ltd, Lockheed Martin and SERCO.

AWE's new Chief Executive, Dr. John Rae, helps raise the AWE Management Ltd flag for the first time on 1 April 2000. ▶

Chapter 12

The original airfield plan is still visible in this 1993 aerial photograph of AWE's Aldermaston site viewed from the North-west.

KEEPING THE PEACE • The Aldermaston Story

A Safe and
GOOD NEIGHBOUR

Chapter 13

A Safe and **Good Neighbour**

One of the corporate goals adopted by AWE's management during the 1990s was to be seen as a safe and good neighbour, in response to increasing calls from local people for more openness, particularly on matters affecting health and safety. To coin a phrase, AWE had not simply to be safe - it had to be seen to be safe. Despite the more reticent approach of the Cold War years, safety had always been a priority, with the UKAEA having had a strong radiation safety culture from the beginning. But with increasingly stringent levels of radiation protection being required by the Regulatory authorities, continuous improvement was essential.

A key impetus to safety improvements was the report by Sir Edward Pochin into radiological health and safety at Aldermaston, which had been published in 1978. Pochin was a world famous radiologist whose experience of nuclear weapons work went back to the US weapons tests in 1946 at Bikini, in which he had taken part. Pochin had been asked to carry out the work after routine monitoring indicated that three women working in Aldermaston's laundry appeared to have levels of plutonium in their lungs in excess of the level recommended by the International Commission on Radiological Protection.

Pochin found that, whilst emissions to the environment posed no hazard to the health of local people, the reliability of health protection measures for the workforce was affected due to inadequate staffing in the key areas of health physics and maintenance. He recommended that staff levels in these areas be increased *'as a matter of some urgency'*. He also found that whilst conditions in most buildings could be improved by simple methods such as improved ventilation, certain buildings presented *'particular problems, especially in containment of radioactivity and of ventilation'*.

The Pochin Report led to major improvements in health and safety, materials handling and waste management. In July 1980, Pochin himself officially opened a Whole Body Monitor at Aldermaston - one of only seven in the country. It was a significant addition to AWE's ability to keep a close watch on the health of its workforce, with up to 2,500 employees a year being routinely scanned.

◀ The Aldermaston site in 1978, showing the open 'Centre Site' area, where a major new plutonium facility was to be built as a result of the Pochin Report, issued that year.

Modern steel - which becomes slightly radioactive during manufacture because of nuclear fallout - could not be used, so steel plates from the 'pre-nuclear' cruiser HMS *Lion* were used in the construction.

The most significant change resulting from Pochin was to Aldermaston's 'centre site' area. For decades it had remained a green oasis amongst the office blocks, workshops and laboratories. This became the location for the new plutonium processing facility known as A90. This was Aldermaston's biggest ever capital project, with construction and commissioning spread over fifteen years and construction costs of £460M. A90 became fully operational in 1998 - the world's most modern plutonium handling facility.

Since the 1970s, growing environmental awareness had led to improvements in waste management, in particular leading to major reductions in the volume and contamination level of radioactive waste and the construction of purpose built waste stores. One of the problems facing Aldermaston has been the lack of a national repository for so-called Intermediate Level Waste. Until a suitable site has been identified this waste, comprising such items as filters and material from decommissioning

▼ Sir Edward Pochin opens Aldermaston's Whole Body Monitor in July 1980. The Director, Colin Fielding, looks on.

redundant facilities, has to be stored at Aldermaston. Doing so safely is an important part of AWE's waste management strategy; purpose built intermediate level waste stores now mean that AWE can safely store its wastes until a national repository is available. Planning permission for the construction of a further store was granted in 1999 which will provide extra capacity for the waste arising from the decommissioning programme.

In July 1989, a severe rainstorm swept across southern England: Aldermaston stood in its path.

Chapter 13

One of the modern Intermediate Level Waste stores at Aldermaston. The waste includes such items as filters and material from decommissioning works.

KEEPING THE PEACE • The Aldermaston story

Water draining from the site northwards towards the Kennet valley passed through a series of ponds, which originally were an ornamental feature of the grounds of Aldermaston Court. Unable to contain the deluge, the ponds overflowed into a larger lake at Aldermaston Court and onwards into the village, the floodwaters demolishing a wall as they went.

Monitoring of a small area of marshland at Aldermaston Court, then owned by Blue Circle Cement, showed slightly raised levels of radiation and AWE embarked on a major exercise to remove the soil and return the site to its original state. This incident gave added impetus to a scheme already under consideration to improve water management in the North Ponds area and in September 1996 a multi-million pound civil engineering scheme got under way to provide sufficient water storage capacity to deal with a 'hundred year' flood. The new scheme was in operation by 1999.

During the 1990s construction of new buildings ensured that AWE's business could be conducted not only more efficiently but in line with modern safety practice. A purpose built emergency response centre was opened in 1997; in the same year a waste transfer station opened to improve the handling and disposal of non-radioactive waste such as paints and batteries and a new explosives laboratory opened in 1998, replacing a number of obsolescent facilities. In the following year a new facility was commissioned to handle the radioactive gas tritium.

Aldermaston's North Ponds water management system was commissioned in 1999; it controls discharges into local watercourses and is capable of dealing with a 'hundred year' flood.

Chapter 13

The conversion of the coal fired boiler house to gas in 1995 not only reduced the road traffic needed to deliver some 40,000 tonnes of coal per year to the site, it significantly reduced Aldermaston's emissions to the environment. The decommissioning of old or redundant facilities not only helped reduce energy use but provided a more attractive workplace. From a total of more than 1,300 buildings, AWE's 1998 rationalization plan aimed at reducing this to 870 by 2002.

Today, AWE must comply with the stringent requirements of its Nuclear Site Licence. Awarded in July 1997, the issue of the Licence by the Nuclear Installations Inspectorate was the culmination of two years' intensive work. Licensing was of profound importance for AWE; it ushered in a new era of accountability, making AWE more open to independent review and audit than ever before. The licence required AWE to comply with thirty-five conditions covering the whole range of its activities, such as safe working practices, emergency preparedness and disposal of waste. Detailed 'safety cases' were prepared for all major operations, many of them breaking new ground. In all, preparation for nuclear site licensing cost more than £60M. It was a genuinely Herculean task, made possible only by the sheer dedication and professionalism of AWE's workforce, with support from specialist contractors where necessary.

Additional regulation of AWE's activities is carried out by the Environment Agency, which sets the levels of discharges to the environment and the Ministry of Agriculture Fisheries and Food, which carries out its own monitoring of AWE's impact on the environment. Within this regulatory framework the safety of the workforce, the public and the environment remains AWE's highest priority.

Since contractorization, increasing emphasis was placed on safety; fundamental to this was the introduction of a 'safety related incident' reporting system in 1993, with employees encouraged to report all incidents, however minor. In addition techniques are used to keep the exposure of the workforce to radiation and other hazards as low as reasonably practicable. This not only resulted in real improvements in health and safety performance, it won external recognition from the Royal Society for the Prevention of Accidents (RoSPA), with gold awards for occupational safety being presented for 1997 and 1998.

Although nuclear licensing provided a sharp regulatory focus, AWE's releases of waste material had long been subject to independent control, under the provisions of the 1960 Radioactive Substances Act, with Inspectors having access to make independent measurements and samples being analysed at the Laboratory of the Government Chemist. The argument that AWE could avoid regulation under 'Crown Immunity' had never really held good.

Parts of the Aldermaston site are havens for wildlife. Here, a member of AWE's angling society enjoys the peaceful surroundings of the Decoy Pond.

Chapter 13

Since being awarded the management contract in 1993, Hunting-BRAE Ltd developed AWE's community relations activities, ushering in a new age of openness. We have seen that in the early days, an attitude of resigned acceptance greeted the establishment of a nuclear factory in the midst of a pleasant swathe of Berkshire countryside. By the late 1950s, organizations such as CND had begun to challenge the whole concept of nuclear deterrence. And in the Cold War atmosphere of the following decades it was understandable that a cloak of secrecy should descend over almost every aspect of life 'behind the wire' at Aldermaston.

One of the first examples of the spirit of openness which followed contractorization was AWE's agreement to give evidence at a 'community enquiry' into safety at AWE, held by Reading Borough Council. The creation of a Local Liaison Committee enabled local community representatives to meet AWE's managers face to face and to debate matters of mutual concern, while a new willingness to speak to the local media led to more balanced reporting of AWE's affairs.

The late 1990s were also characterized by a recognition of the fact that, during almost sixty years of operation as an airfield and a nuclear weapons factory, there was an environmental legacy which needed attention. An Environmental Improvement Programme was launched in 1997. This revealed that initial surveys had identified areas both on the Aldermaston site and in the near vicinity, where there were traces of organic solvents, plutonium and mercury from past operations. Although there was no evidence to suggest that they posed any threat to employees or the public, AWE undertook to carry out remedial measures where necessary.

In addition, AWE commissioned Southampton University to conduct an off-site survey of radioactive contamination. A Scientific Information Group was set up with local government authorities to ensure independence and public access to the findings. The first report was issued in June 1999 and concluded that, although small amounts of contamination had been found, they posed no significant radiological risk.

The impact of nuclear facilities on local people and the environment is naturally a matter of great concern. It came into particular focus in 1983 when a Yorkshire Television programme suggested there was a higher than expected level of childhood cancers in the vicinity of the BNFL plant at Sellafield. Studies of particular relevance to Aldermaston were carried out by the National Radiological Protection Board in 1986, by haematologists at Reading's Royal Berkshire Hospital in 1988 and by the Committee on the Medical Aspects of Radiation in the Environment (COMARE) in 1989. The findings showed that, whilst there was a small excess of childhood cancers in the Aldermaston and Burghfield area, discharges from the sites were too low to explain it.

During the 1990s, AWE participated in the Nuclear Industry Family Study, which published its first report in May 1999. This found a statistical link between the occurrence of leukaemia in children and fathers with a high preconception radiation dose, but was based on only three cases from the many thousands of radiation workers covered by the study. Despite the vast amount of research, no conclusive evidence has yet emerged to explain the cause of cancer clusters. It is an area in which AWE takes a close interest and a Health Effects Group was set up in 1997 specifically to examine those concerns.

Involvement in local charities and links with local schools formed an important part of AWE's community programme during the late 1990s. Special help was given to the SeeAbility project to build a home for young people with Juvenile Batten's Disease. The charity was able to purchase the site of William Penney's former home in Tadley, Heather House. The new centre, also called Heather House, was opened by Lady Penney in 1998, so maintaining a fifty year link with Aldermaston.

In another initiative, AWE's graduate trainees worked with two local schools to design new science laboratories and organized a successful Schools' Engineering Challenge which annually draws entries from more than twenty local secondary schools. Taken together, these activities have helped to demystify an organization which for too long had remained apart from the community it had helped create.

Members of the Southampton University Geosciences team take soil samples close to AWE's Aldermaston site in 1997. The results of the surveys have been shared with local councils

Chapter 13

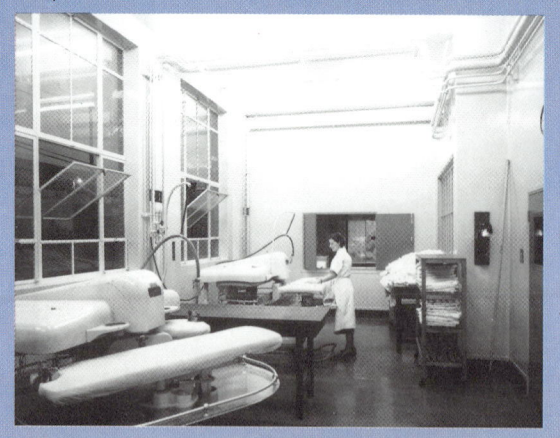

◀ AWRE Aldermaston's laundry in 1952. The Pochin report of 1978 identified the need for improved radiation safety practice in such facilities.

▼ Young visitors to an AWE Families' Day get to grips with protective clothing and monitoring equipment.

▲ The Pochin Report recommended a number of safety improvements. One outcome was the construction of a modern plutonium research and component manufacturing facility, seen here during the building phase in 1986.

▲ Lady Penney, the widow of AWRE's first director, lays the foundation stone of Heather House, a new centre for the charity SeeAbility, built on the site of their former home in Tadley.

▶ Members of the AWE Local Liaison Committee visit Aldermaston's new liquid effluent treatment plant in 1998.

▲ In this 1989 picture, Aldermaston's new boiler house is dominated by massive coal stocks. Conversion to gas in 1995 significantly reduced AWE's emissions to the atmosphere.

KEEPING THE PEACE • The Aldermaston Story

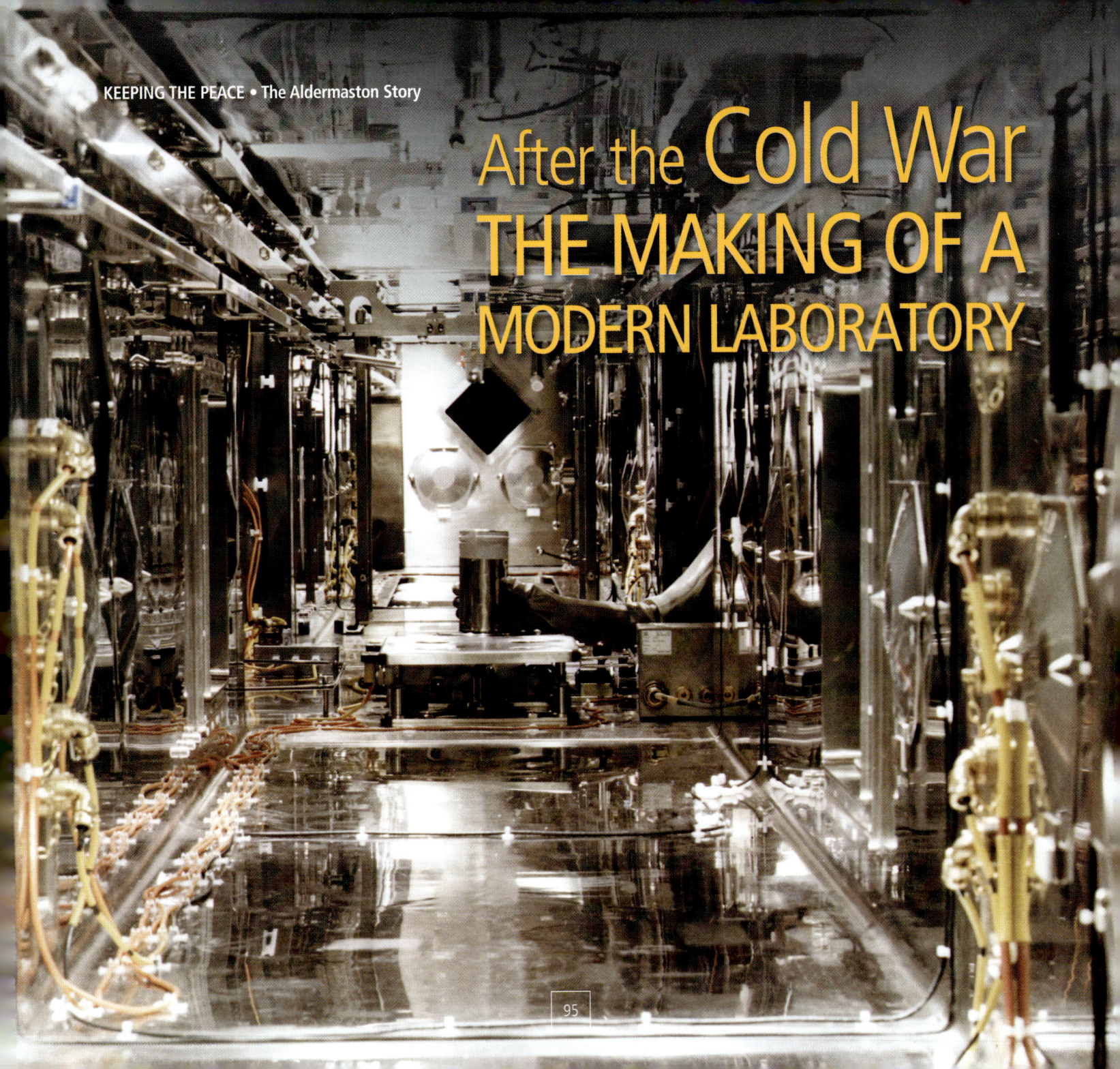

After the Cold War
THE MAKING OF A MODERN LABORATORY

Chapter 14

After the Cold War - **The Making of a modern laboratory**

AWRE was set up in the early days of the Cold War and it was the Cold War which shaped the Aldermaston story for nearly forty years. When it came to a dramatic end in 1989 with the breaching of the Berlin Wall, a new era was heralded. For Aldermaston, the new world order posed fresh and exciting challenges.

The changes in world politics did not mean that Britain could abandon its nuclear capability at a stroke. Although the accelerated programme of withdrawal of nuclear weapons from service had begun in 1992, the results of a comprehensive Strategic Defence Review published in 1998 confirmed the Government's view that Britain continued to require a *'credible and effective minimum nuclear deterrent'* based on the *Trident* submarine force. The Review added: *'For as long as Britain has nuclear forces, we will ensure that we have a robust capability at the Atomic Weapons Establishment to underwrite the safety and reliability of our nuclear warheads without recourse to nuclear testing'*.

◀ A 'transfer tunnel' used for the safe movement of radioactive materials, in the new plutonium processing facility A90.

It is this policy which shapes AWE's principal role today: to maintain *Trident* for its full operational life of between twenty-five and thirty years and to withdraw old weapons like *WE 177* and *Chevaline* from service. AWE is also charged by the Government with maintaining the national capability to design and manufacture a successor warhead if called upon to do so.

With the ending of Britain's underground testing programme at the Nevada Test site in 1991, a vital key to AWE's work in the 1990s and beyond is a range of Above Ground Experiments, known as 'AGEX'. Because AWE can no longer conduct live nuclear tests, its mission has in fact become much more complex. In order to validate the safety and effectiveness of the various detailed design changes which are the inevitable consequence of a system life of thirty years, AWE now operates a science-based stockpile stewardship programme in order to re-certify design, materials and process changes without nuclear testing. It is a radically different task from that of the first forty years, but the challenges are still there, calling for great ingenuity to overcome the problems posed by an ageing warhead and an inability to put theoretical designs to the ultimate test.

AGEX will sustain confidence in the nuclear safety and reliability of Britain's deterrent over the long term, by placing almost total reliance on a range of enhanced laboratory facilities and by conducting trials which simulate nuclear events without the release of nuclear energy. Information from hydrodynamics and laser based plasma physics experiments is processed using greatly improved computers to solve the immensely complex equations which describe a nuclear event. This work is vital to augment the historic data available from past nuclear tests, which provide the 'real' data needed to validate the computer models of the future.

At AWE, the term 'Hydrodynamics' describes the techniques available for measuring the progress of a shock wave through the materials of a simulated nuclear device up to the precise moment of the nuclear explosion. This is not a new process for AWE: Aldermaston's bomb chambers - buildings H1, H2 and H4 - were constructed in the mid 1950s and have been in use ever since. They were designed to contain explosions of up to ten pounds of high explosive, sufficient to achieve a small-scale simulation of the implosion which triggers the nuclear reaction. Now, in a test-less world, this pre-nuclear phase is as far as Aldermaston can go in studying the functioning of a nuclear warhead.

▼ Mogul-E - two such machines generate intense bursts of x-rays which can see into the heart of a simulated implosion of the *Trident* warhead. AWE has an international reputation in this field.

Aldermaston has established a world lead in this specialist field. The facilities known as MOGUL -D (commissioned in 1980) and MOGUL- E (commissioned in 1995), give AWE a unique ability to conduct flash x-radiography shots to look into the heart of the simulated nuclear event. At Aldermaston, the technique is known as 'core punching'. The MOGULS produce intense x-ray pulses lasting less than one ten-millionth of a second, sufficient to 'freeze' the motion of the implosion. Aldermaston achieved the world's first full-scale core punch in 1982. By using MOGUL D

Chapter 14

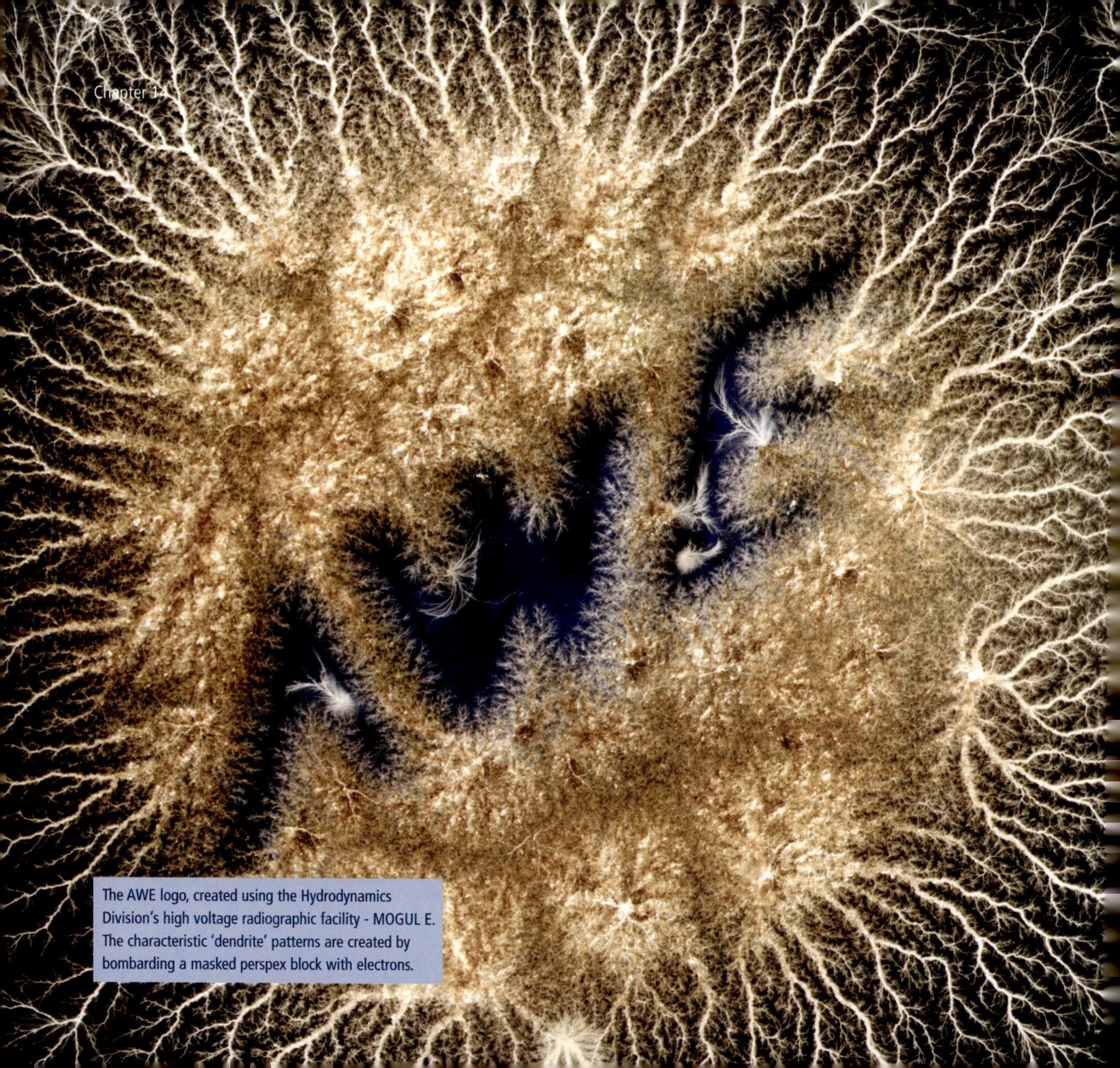

The AWE logo, created using the Hydrodynamics Division's high voltage radiographic facility - MOGUL E. The characteristic 'dendrite' patterns are created by bombarding a masked perspex block with electrons.

KEEPING THE PEACE • The Aldermaston story

and E together, the world's first full scale dual-axis core punch was achieved in 1995, so maintaining Britain's lead over other nuclear nations in this area of research.

Improvements to these facilities are planned which will provide the quality of data needed for calibrating computer models and codes. It is all part of AWE's process for establishing confident predictions of the warhead's safety and performance.

During the 1990s, AWE collaborated in the pioneering US technique of proton radiography, which allowed the examination of particles generated during the later stages of a simulated primary implosion. In 1999, using a device - designed at Aldermaston - called 'Billi-G', AWE's hydrodynamics team took part in a collaborative experiment with the Los Alamos Neutron Science Center, which, for the first time allowed a number of successive images of the implosion event.

Each picture captured a fleeting event lasting just fifty billionths of a second, the whole sequence lasting no more than fifty millionths of a second. This was the first implosion experiment conducted in the US since the last underground test in 1991. This emerging technology offers the prospect of improvements in Aldermaston's ability to diagnose the safety and reliability of the nation's nuclear stockpile.

Dr. John Weale, Head of the Radiation Physics Division, ▶ describes the target chamber to the Queen during her visit to open the HELEN laser on 29 June 1979.

Chapter 14

For twenty years AWE's HELEN laser has contributed vital data in the field of high temperature warhead plasma physics. Opened by the Queen in 1979, it continues to provide an important experimental capability. Although conceived during the Cold War, it is of particular value in a post-test ban treaty era, when there is a clear need for a high power laser to simulate the key physics processes occurring within a thermonuclear weapon.

By generating temperatures of up to three million degrees and pressures of millions of atmospheres, HELEN is capable of simulating the extreme conditions generated within a nuclear warhead. This has enabled AWE to study the individual phenomena occurring within the warhead in order to validate the computer generated predictions.

AWE's scientists have carried out pioneering warhead physics work using HELEN, with the short pulse times (around one billionth of a second) and the sub-millimetre dimensions of the target providing real challenges.

The nuclear test ban brought with it an increased need to study warhead physics. Pioneering work in this field has been the development at Aldermaston of a suite of experiments to study the interplay of radiation with the hydrodynamic evolution of complex targets. The US nuclear laboratories recognized the importance of this work (known as 'The English Concept'), an achievement of which Aldermaston can be justly proud.

Building on the success of HELEN, AWE's scientists have defined the requirements for a much more powerful laser which can bring the new concept to fruition. To achieve this they will be working with American colleagues at the National Ignition Facility laser currently under construction at the Lawrence Livermore National Laboratory in California.

The lack of computational power in the 1950s led to the under performance of some trial warhead designs. The Ferranti Mk1* installed in April 1955 would be greatly outperformed by the simplest personal computer today. Now, AWE has computer power far greater than could have been envisaged forty years ago. By exploiting the huge amounts of data that can be derived from the AGEX programme and relating them to existing data from underground tests, AWE can face future challenges with greater confidence.

A major step forward in the 1990s has been the development of numerical simulations of dynamic processes in three dimensions. This is essential not only for nuclear safety assessments, but also to evaluate the effects on warhead performance of the imperfections which occur in the real world of

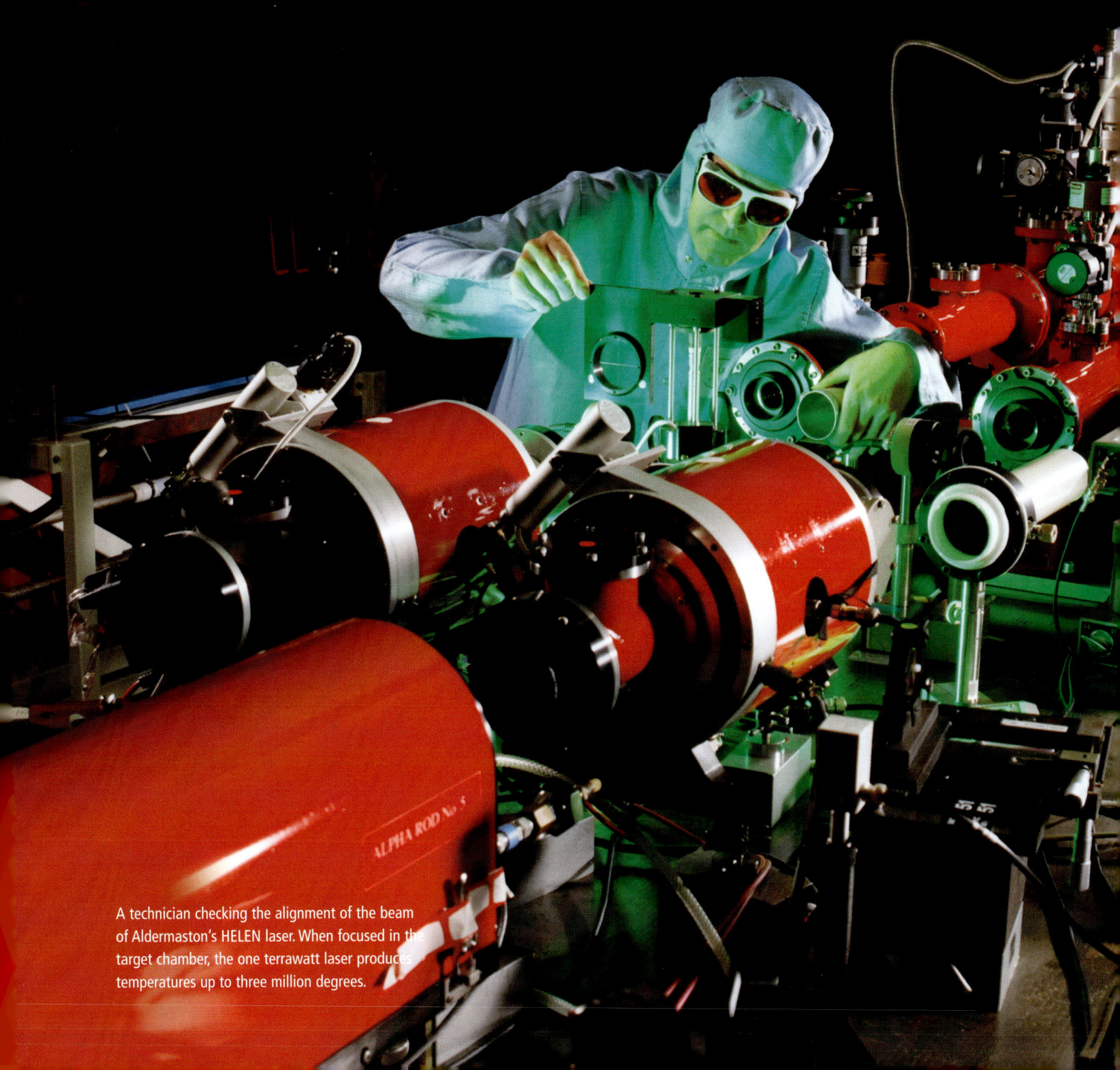

A technician checking the alignment of the beam of Aldermaston's HELEN laser. When focused in the target chamber, the one terrawatt laser produces temperatures up to three million degrees.

Chapter 14

manufacture and assembly and which may tend to worsen as the warhead ages. Only by recourse to 'massively parallel processing' can such calculations be made in a realistic timescale.

AWE entered this era in 1996; in 1998 an upgrade of the IBM RS6000 parallel processor was an important step towards achieving the computing power AWE will need fully to support *Trident* in the coming decades - a vital part of the science-based stockpile stewardship programme.

In parallel with developments in science and computing, there have been similar advances in the fields of engineering and materials. These, too, are essential if AWE is to assure the long term performance of the weapon.

During the five decades of the nuclear programme, materials science, chemistry and engineering have been at the heart of Aldermaston's work and continue to be so. The ability to 'characterize' materials, that is to understand their properties and performance as they age over the lifetime of the warhead and to assess how those changes might affect its performance are vital to the effective maintenance of the stockpile.

Aldermaston is now developing techniques for modelling the behaviour of materials down to the molecular scale; this not only improves scientists' understanding of how compounds such as polymers might degrade over time, it can add to their appreciation of how a complex component might be affected by the changes occurring in each of its parts. And in the design of those components, virtual prototypes can now be generated at the early stages of a project; AWE can evaluate complex new designs without having to manufacture them, so avoiding the need for difficult or expensive actual testing.

Virtual prototyping is set to become an important part of the *Trident* programme; by maintaining close links between designers, engineering analysts and environmental test engineers during project development, AWE can be confident that the warhead will continue to meet its operational requirements.

The skills developed at Aldermaston over half a century are now proving to be of global importance and have presented AWE with an opportunity to develop new objectives. For example, the science of forensic seismology has been developed over many years and AWE has become a world leader in distinguishing between man-made underground explosions and natural events such as earthquakes.

This work was of particular importance during negotiations towards a Comprehensive Test Ban Treaty in Geneva between 1994 and 1996, and in 1998, when AWE's scientists were well equipped to

KEEPING THE PEACE • The Aldermaston story

offer expert and timely advice to the Ministry of Defence on the underground nuclear tests carried out by India and Pakistan.

With the Cold War consigned to history, the need to verify the reduction and elimination of nuclear weapons is of growing importance. Following an eighteen-month long study, early in the millennium year 2000, AWE presented the Ministry of Defence with a report on its proposals for an integrated Threat Reduction Programme. Key elements of this will be threat assessment, verifying compliance with international treaties, controlling national stocks of nuclear materials and crisis response.

In the field of arms control and reduction, AWE is developing techniques for the scientific authentication and tracking of nuclear warheads and the measurement of the radiological 'signatures' of facilities involved in nuclear weapons production. A research programme aimed at advising the Government on how to achieve a verifiable test ban regime has also been set up.

In 1997 the changed world political scene was demonstrated in a practical way when AWE supplied 400 armoured 'supercontainers' to support the internationally sponsored withdrawal of nuclear weapons from the former USSR states to the Russian Federation. In 1999, AWE made the first shipment of weapons grade plutonium to storage under the control of the International Atomic Energy Agency's safeguards.

Welcome as these developments are, they could scarcely have been foreseen fifty years ago when Aldermaston's weapons capability was forged in the chill winds of the Cold War.

Peter Marshall, one of AWE's forensic seismologists with a seismogram showing global earth movements recorded at Blacknest. Below is the seismic trace result of the Indian underground nuclear test on 11 May 1998.

Chapter 14

◀ A modern facility for the safe and secure storage of radioactive material, part of the extensive modernization of AWE undertaken during the 1990s.

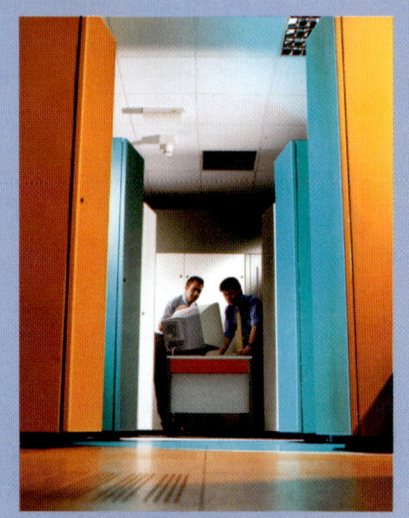

▶ AWE's latest high performance computer, the IBM RS6000SP, installed in 1996 and since updated. Using massively parallel processing technology, its role is increasingly important to AWE's capability to underwrite the safety and reliability of the warhead stockpile.

▲ One aspect of the end of the Cold War has been the assistance given to the former Soviet Union. Here, final checks are being made to one of 400 armoured supercontainers supplied by AWE to support the internationally sponsored withdrawal of nuclear weapons to Russia from the former USSR states.

▲ AWE is developing techniques to detect the presence of nuclear warheads and measure the radiological 'signatures' of nuclear weapons facilities. The aim is to ensure that AWE has a national capability to contribute to the global arms reduction verification process.

▲ AWE now has some of the world's most modern facilities for the safe handling of radioactive materials, such as this glove box suite in building A90.

◀ The Control console of AWRE's IBM 704 computer, installed in 1957. Despite its memory of only 8k words, it played an important role in evaluating the design of the devices tested on the *Grapple* series of nuclear tests. The IBM RS6000SP installed some forty years later is ten million times more powerful.

KEEPING THE PEACE • The Aldermaston Story

Towards the Next 50 years

Chapter 15

Towards the next fifty years

The skill and dedication of AWE's employees has always been one of its great strengths; the scientists and engineers who worked tirelessly to produce and successfully test Britain's first nuclear device and who went on to develop a range of stockpile warheads as well as the experimental and test equipment which supported them, were undoubtedly at the leading edge of their profession.

Equipping people for the future has always been of importance at AWE. Aldermaston's Apprentice School can boast a long tradition of training young engineers, some of whom have gone on to hold senior positions. The training of apprentices in all branches of engineering began at Aldermaston in 1952 and by the early 1960s about one hundred and seventy boys were under training. At this time, many apprentices lived at the Boundary Hall hostel where, according to a brochure of the time: '..the welfare of the boys is under the guidance of a YMCA warden'. The scheme has always aimed to provide a rounded education, with sport and adventurous training courses taking their place alongside acquiring technical skills. By the end of 1999, some two thousand trainees, both young men and women, had passed through the Apprentice School.

AWE's apprentices have played a role in community affairs, too; a particular speciality has been the repair of clocks, with Ashford Hill Church, Heath End Village Hall and Baughurst Community Hall being recent beneficiaries.

◀ One of AWE's graduate trainees with pupils at the Willink School, Burghfield Common. Graduate trainees have produced designs for science laboratories at a number of local schools; this is an important part of their training, which in turn ensures that AWE maintains its vital base of skills and knowledge for the future.

▲ AWE's apprentices with the clock at Ashford Hill church, which they restored in 1998.

KEEPING THE PEACE • The Aldermaston story

In its Strategic Plan issued in 1999, which looked forward to the year 2010, AWE recognized the importance of its becoming the 'employer of choice' for scientists, engineers, trades and business people, as well as being a sought after partner in collaborative science and technology projects.

Fundamental to this approach is AWE's Graduate Trainee scheme and a wide range of training, development and further education opportunities,

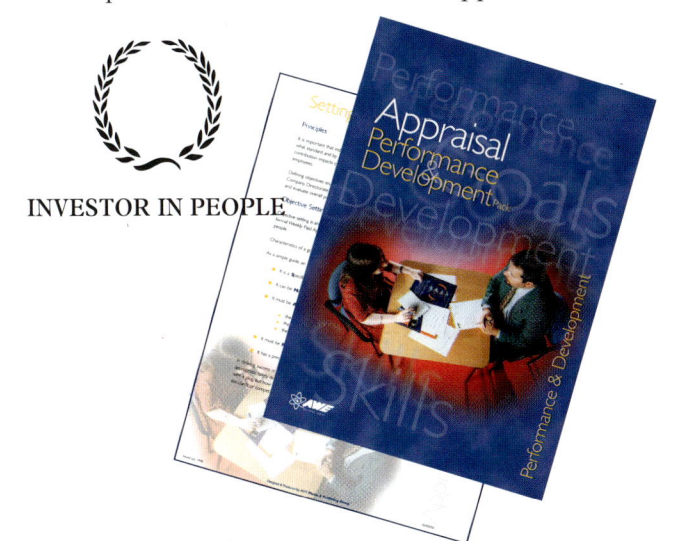

INVESTOR IN PEOPLE

▲ AWE was officially recognized as an 'Investor in People' in March 2000. This is an internationally respected standard which should bring long term benefits as AWE enters the twenty-first century.

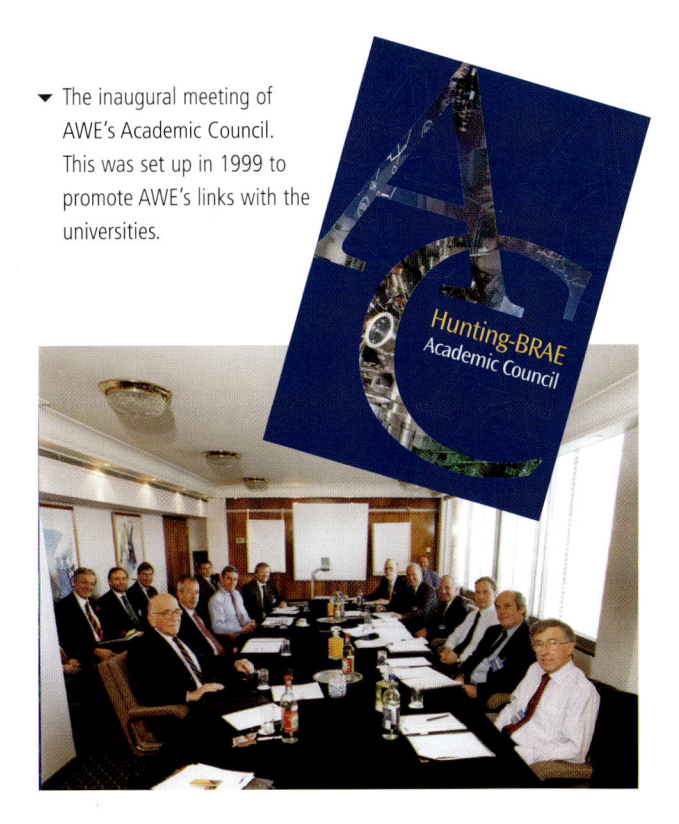

▼ The inaugural meeting of AWE's Academic Council. This was set up in 1999 to promote AWE's links with the universities.

all geared to realizing the potential of the staff. During 1998 1,525 employees attended external training and 360 were sponsored by AWE to attend further education. Links with universities were strengthened through the Academic Council formed in 1998, which comprises senior academics and industrialists, with the aim of advising AWE on suitable areas for future research.

Chapter 15

AWE is committed to supporting the *Trident* warhead throughout its operational life, which will be well into the twenty-first century.

KEEPING THE PEACE • The Aldermaston story

In March 2000, AWE was formally recognized as an 'Investor in People', reflecting achievement in communications, training and development. Together with the William Penney Post Graduate Fellowships, the first five of which were awarded in 1999, these innovations should ensure that AWE continues to attract the brightest and the best.

But underlying the new and exciting developments of recent years, the mission is the same now as it was fifty years ago - a singular purpose to provide, maintain and certify the UK's nuclear deterrent, but with the added challenge of developing arms control verification techniques.

AWE's new managing contractor - AWE Management Limited - are committed to supporting the *Trident* stockpile and to maintaining national capability. Coupled with the vision to achieve world standards of excellence in innovative science and technology, and with a range of strategic imperatives designed to achieve those aims, Aldermaston stands well placed to enter its next half-century.

AWE has organized a number of international conferences, including one on materials ageing, held at St. Catherine's College Oxford in 1999. Understanding the ageing of materials is of great importance in enabling AWE to maintain the *Trident* warhead safely and effectively into the twenty-first century.

Chapter 15

Engineering training from the 1950s to the present day. Many of AWE's apprentices have gone on to hold senior positions.

In its 'Strategy 2000' document, AWEML identified its strategic imperatives; these include achieving effective research and development programmes to meet current and future requirements for nuclear warheads, whilst being world class in environment health and safety performance.

The Aldermaston Learning Facility (ALF) was opened in February 1995; it forms part of AWE's Employee Development Programme and is an important tool for preparing staff to meet the challenges of the future.

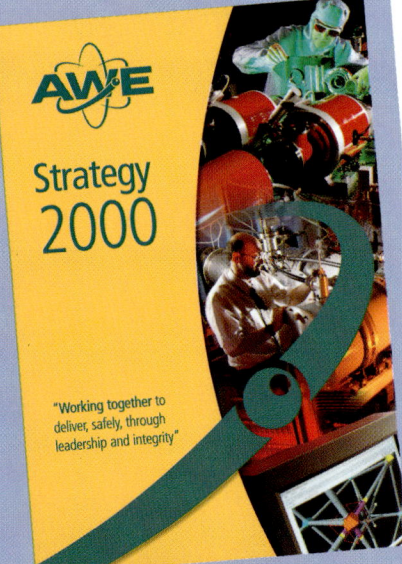

The house journal *AWE Today* provides employees and their families with a wide range of news and features on the work of AWE past, present and future.

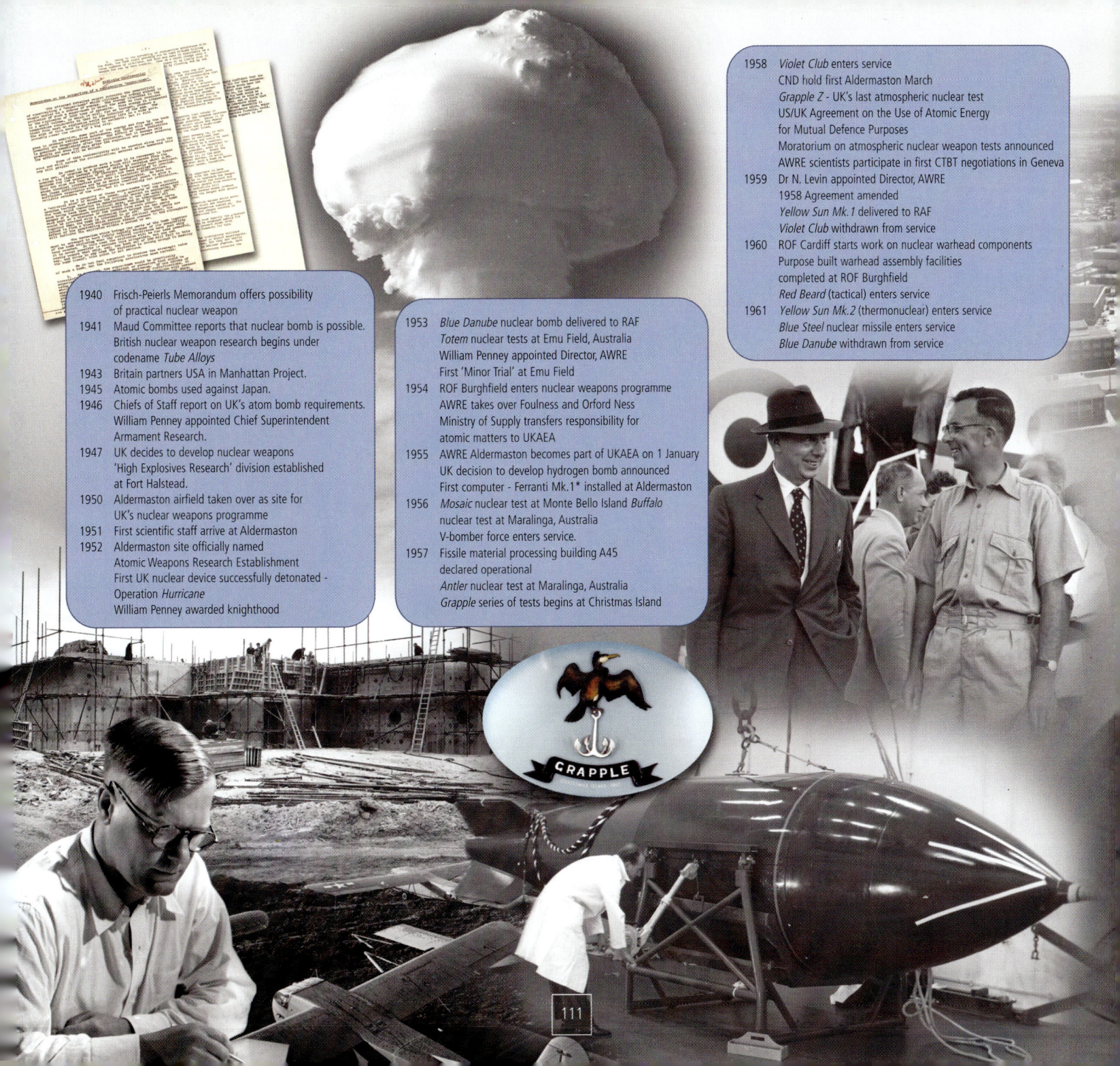

1940	Frisch-Peierls Memorandum offers possibility of practical nuclear weapon
1941	Maud Committee reports that nuclear bomb is possible. British nuclear weapon research begins under codename *Tube Alloys*
1943	Britain partners USA in Manhattan Project.
1945	Atomic bombs used against Japan.
1946	Chiefs of Staff report on UK's atom bomb requirements. William Penney appointed Chief Superintendent Armament Research.
1947	UK decides to develop nuclear weapons 'High Explosives Research' division established at Fort Halstead.
1950	Aldermaston airfield taken over as site for UK's nuclear weapons programme
1951	First scientific staff arrive at Aldermaston
1952	Aldermaston site officially named Atomic Weapons Research Establishment First UK nuclear device successfully detonated - Operation *Hurricane* William Penney awarded knighthood
1953	*Blue Danube* nuclear bomb delivered to RAF *Totem* nuclear tests at Emu Field, Australia William Penney appointed Director, AWRE First 'Minor Trial' at Emu Field
1954	ROF Burghfield enters nuclear weapons programme AWRE takes over Foulness and Orford Ness Ministry of Supply transfers responsibility for atomic matters to UKAEA
1955	AWRE Aldermaston becomes part of UKAEA on 1 January UK decision to develop hydrogen bomb announced First computer - Ferranti Mk.1* installed at Aldermaston
1956	*Mosaic* nuclear test at Monte Bello Island *Buffalo* nuclear test at Maralinga, Australia V-bomber force enters service.
1957	Fissile material processing building A45 declared operational *Antler* nuclear test at Maralinga, Australia *Grapple* series of tests begins at Christmas Island
1958	*Violet Club* enters service CND hold first Aldermaston March *Grapple Z* - UK's last atmospheric nuclear test US/UK Agreement on the Use of Atomic Energy for Mutual Defence Purposes Moratorium on atmospheric nuclear weapon tests announced AWRE scientists participate in first CTBT negotiations in Geneva
1959	Dr N. Levin appointed Director, AWRE 1958 Agreement amended *Yellow Sun Mk.1* delivered to RAF *Violet Club* withdrawn from service
1960	ROF Cardiff starts work on nuclear warhead components Purpose built warhead assembly facilities completed at ROF Burghfield *Red Beard* (tactical) enters service
1961	*Yellow Sun Mk.2* (thermonuclear) enters service *Blue Steel* nuclear missile enters service *Blue Danube* withdrawn from service

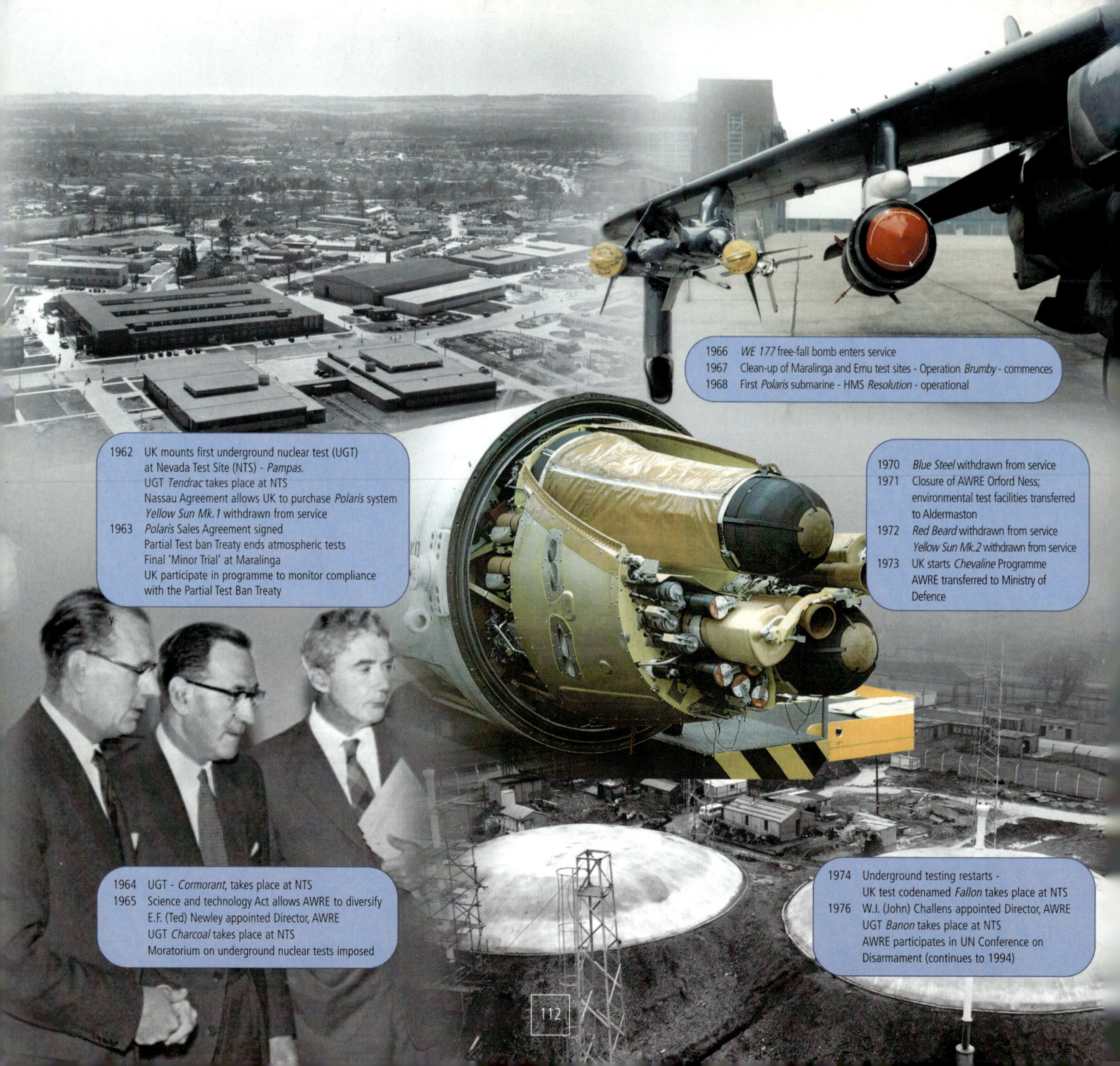

1962	UK mounts first underground nuclear test (UGT) at Nevada Test Site (NTS) - *Pampas*. UGT *Tendrac* takes place at NTS Nassau Agreement allows UK to purchase *Polaris* system *Yellow Sun Mk.1* withdrawn from service
1963	*Polaris* Sales Agreement signed Partial Test ban Treaty ends atmospheric tests Final 'Minor Trial' at Maralinga UK participate in programme to monitor compliance with the Partial Test Ban Treaty
1964	UGT - *Cormorant*, takes place at NTS
1965	Science and technology Act allows AWRE to diversify E.F. (Ted) Newley appointed Director, AWRE UGT *Charcoal* takes place at NTS Moratorium on underground nuclear tests imposed
1966	*WE 177* free-fall bomb enters service
1967	Clean-up of Maralinga and Emu test sites - Operation *Brumby* - commences
1968	First *Polaris* submarine - HMS *Resolution* - operational
1970	*Blue Steel* withdrawn from service
1971	Closure of AWRE Orford Ness; environmental test facilities transferred to Aldermaston
1972	*Red Beard* withdrawn from service *Yellow Sun Mk.2* withdrawn from service
1973	UK starts *Chevaline* Programme AWRE transferred to Ministry of Defence
1974	Underground testing restarts - UK test codenamed *Fallon* takes place at NTS
1976	W.J. (John) Challens appointed Director, AWRE UGT *Banon* takes place at NTS AWRE participates in UN Conference on Disarmament (continues to 1994)

1977	AWRE provides technical advice on detection of underground tests to US/USSR/UK trilateral negotiations
1978	Pochin Report recommends improved safety procedures
	David Cardwell appointed Director AWRE
1979	First CRAY supercomputer installed
	HELEN laser opened by HM the Queen
	UGT *Nessel* takes place at NTS
1980	UK Government announces decision to produce *Trident*
	MOGUL-D commissioned
	Whole Body monitor opened by Sir E. Pochin
	Colin Fielding appointed Director AWRE
	Trident sales agreement signed
	UGTs *Colwick*, *Dutchess* and *Serpa* take place at NTS
	First *Chevaline* warheads enter stockpile
1981	Design work for new plutonium facility - A90 - begins
	UGT *Rousanne* takes place at NTS
1982	P.G.E.F. (Peter) Jones appointed Director AWRE
	UGT *Gibne* takes place at NTS
1983	Construction of A90 begins
	Polaris A3 withdrawn from service
	Design work for building A89 begins
1984	UGTs *Mundo* and *Egmont* take place at NTS
1985	Construction of building A89 starts
	UGT *Kinibito* takes place at NTS
1986	UGT *Darwin* takes place at NTS
1987	AWRE becomes Atomic Weapons Establishment (AWE)
	ROF Burghfield and ROF Cardiff subsumed under AWE management
	T.P. (Tom) McLean apppointed Director AWE
	UGT *Midland* takes place at NTS
1988	National Radiological Board issue stricter radiation protection guidelines
1989	Government announces AWE to be 'contractorized'
1990	Hunting-BRAE Ltd. awarded Phase 1 management contract
	B.H. (Brian) Richards appointed Chief Executive, AWE
	UGT *Houston* takes place at NTS
1991	Death of Lord Penney
	AWE Bill receives Royal Assent, paving way for full contractorization
	UGT *Bristol* takes place at NTS. The UK's final nuclear test
1992	AWE produce 10-year Waste Management Plan
1993	Hunting-BRAE Ltd. awarded Phase 2 management contract
	AWE receives ISO 9001 quality accreditation
	First meeting of Aldermaston and Burghfield Local Liaison Committee
1994	First *Trident* submarine - HMS *Vanguard* - enters service
	A.J. (Andrew) Glasgow appointed Chief Executive AWE
	Government announce intention to licence AWE under the Nuclear Installations Act.
	CTBT negotiations begin in Geneva: AWE provides advice on verification and On-site Inspection
1995	MOGUL-E commissioned
	Cray C98D super computer installed
	Chevaline withdrawn from service
1996	Comprehensive Test Ban Treaty signed

1998	*WE 177* withdrawn from service
	Plutonium facility A90 fully operational
	New explosives analysis facility opened at Aldermaston
	Academic Council set up
	Creation of William Penney Fellowships
	IBM RS 6000 computer gives AWE massively parallel processing capability
	UK ratifies CTBT
	Patent granted for development of calixarene molecules
1999	AWE transports first shipment of weapons grade plutonium to storage under IAEA safeguards
	North Ponds water management system commissioned
	Patent granted for fabrication of boron carbide
2000	Fiftieth anniversary of opening of AWRE Aldermaston
	AWE Management Ltd win management contract
	Dr. J. (John) Rae appointed Chief Executive AWE

AWE
MISSION
To provide the national capability for nuclear warheads

VISION
To be recognised for world standards of excellence in innovative science and technology

1997	AWE publishes first Land Quality Survey report
	NII grant nuclear site licences for Aldermaston and Burghfield
	AWE Cardiff closes
	AWE withdraws from Foulness
	R.A. (Robin) Bradley appointed Chief Executive AWE
	400 'Supercontainers' supplied by AWE to Russian Federation
	AWE scientists participate in CTBT Preparatory Commission